'8 6

Hospitality Management
A Capstone Course

Hospitality Management
A Capstone Course

Matt A. Casado
Northern Arizona University

Executive Editor: Vernon R. Anthony
Editorial Assistant: Beth Dyke
Senior Marketing Manager: Ryan DeGrote
Senior Marketing Coordinator: Elizabeth Farrell
Marketing Assistant: Les Roberts
Director of Manufacturing and
   Production: Bruce Johnson
Managing Editor: Mary Carnis
Production Liaison: Jane Bonnell

Production Editor: Shelley Creager
Manufacturing Manager: Ilene Sanford
Manufacturing Buyer: Cathleen Petersen
Creative Director: Cheryl Asherman
Senior Design Coordinator: Miguel Ortiz
Cover Designer: Amy Rosen
Cover Photograph: Janet Christie,
   Getty Images/Photodisc Green

Copyright © 2012 by: Matt A. Casado

ISBN: 1-4699-3028-5
ISBN-13:   9781469930282

To Ann Pistolesi, who likes to read my books

Contents

List of Operational Situations

List of Cases

Preface

The purpose of *Hospitality Management: A Capstone Course* is to provide instructors of senior seminar courses with the necessary tools to teach the last class of the hospitality curriculum. Usually offered in the last semester before graduation, this capstone course is aimed at preparing students for joining the industry, generally as manager-trainees. In most cases, students in senior seminars have completed the majority of their professional, core, and general education course requirements. As part of these courses, they have worked on numerous projects outside the classroom, have listened to industry guest speakers, and have conducted several in situ property inspections. At this time in their education, students are actively interviewing for jobs or have already been hired by companies.

Because senior seminar students often have difficulty staying on task in the classroom but need to be primed for their imminent job entry into the industry, I recommend what might be called a workshop approach that follows topic discussions in class and encourages the resolution of applied cases through groupings of students of mixed ability. The operational situations and cases provided throughout this book illustrate real-life challenges and decisions that lower- and mid-level managers face.

The senior seminar offers the last opportunity for students to review, refine, and demonstrate the essential skills needed to get a job and to succeed in the industry, from competency in creative problem-solving, critical thinking, and effective oral and written communication to ethical reasoning, quantitative analyses, and the use of technology. After all, the majority of students will have to put these concepts into practice in a very short period of time.

Graduate business programs with an emphasis in hospitality can use this book as an introduction to graduate courses. The book could provide a useful compendium of the knowledge necessary to access graduate-level courses for students joining these programs on completion of a bachelor's degree or on entering the program directly from the industry.

Although it is not intended as a test tool or as an in-depth and comprehensive study, the book can nevertheless be used as a pragmatic means for the assessment of hospitality college programs by requiring students to keep individual portfolios of work performed in the senior seminar class. Thus, hotel and restaurant management administrators can obtain academic feedback to measure the outcomes of their programs of study. From the information gathered, program directors can readjust curricular contents and teaching methods to improve instruction.

The book is divided into two parts. Part 1 focuses on initial operating supervisory experiences and quantitative issues that graduates will face on joining the industry. Part 2 involves students in the discussion and resolution of problem-solving strategies, critical thinking, communication skills, and managerial techniques in which they will need to be proficient as they progress in their career after the initial on-the-field training period. The 15 chapters that form the core of this book correspond to the subjects taught in most hotel and restaurant programs. Each chapter includes a list of objectives, an overview, and a variety of practical operational situations or cases that reflect the types of problems and experiences students will face in their first years in the hospitality industry.

I have compiled these examples from my own experience, gained in an extensive career as hotelier and as an instructor of senior seminar classes. The situations and cases are intended for discussion and resolution in the classroom. For this reason, most of them are concise and aimed at preparing students to deal with operational and low-level management situations common in functional areas of the hospitality industry. Teachers of this course will be provided with an instructor's manual that includes a teaching note for each chapter and detailed resolutions of the operational situations and cases.

I would like to thank my wife, Mary, the first reader of my work, and the following reviewers of the original manuscript for their helpful suggestions: Linda J. Shea, University of Massachusetts, Amherst; Eva M. Smith, Spartanburg Technical College; Diane Withrow, Cape Fear Community College; and Steven E. Carlomusto, Johnson and Wales University.

About the Author

Matt A. Casado is professor in the School of Hotel and Restaurant Management at Northern Arizona University. He holds a master's degree in education and a doctorate degree in educational leadership with an emphasis in higher education. A veteran of the hospitality industry, he trained in Switzerland and England before managing operations in Spain and in the United States. He has taught hospitality operations at the university level since 1988, and he has published articles in hospitality and tourism journals, such as the *Cornell H.R.A. Quarterly, Journal of Travel Research, FIU Hospitality Review, Journal of Hospitality and Tourism Education, International Journal of Hospitality Management,* and in national and international industry trade magazines. His experiences as senior seminar course instructor have been instrumental in the writing of this book.

PART 1

Initial Operating Experiences in the Hospitality Industry

Chapter 1

Obtaining a Management-Training Position

CHAPTER OBJECTIVES

- Develop strategies to plan a career in the hospitality industry.
- Identify the best ways to contact prospective employers.
- Understand the role of your college's career services.
- Prepare a perfect resume and cover letter.
- Understand what the first and second interview means.
- Understand what to look for in a job offer.

OVERVIEW

This chapter explains the strategies necessary to obtain a management-training position in the hospitality industry. Students will be able to contact prospective employers directly or by using their college's career services. A perfect resume is indispensable in the search for a job. If the resume is sent by mail or submitted electronically, it should be accompanied by a cover letter explaining the purpose of the application. Students should also have a list of references to be provided to interested employers on request. The chapter also explains how to be successful at the time of interviewing for a position and how to select the most appropriate job offer.

STRATEGIES FOR PLANNING A CAREER IN THE HOSPITALITY INDUSTRY

The hospitality industry offers numerous career opportunities. The majority of job openings are in restaurants and in food and beverage and rooms divisions of lodging operations. Fewer positions are likely to be found in other departments, such as accounting, and sales and marketing that operate with a smaller staff. It is therefore advisable for job seekers to accept any initial management-training job that is offered after an interview. By accepting a position in housekeeping, for instance, the candidate will start getting experience in on-the-job management techniques with that company. After the training period, new employees usually have opportunities to explore other positions that may better fit their personalities, values, interests, and aspirations.

Some students may want to work solely in one aspect of the hospitality industry—for example, in restaurants rather than in hotels. If it turns out that they cannot find a position with a restaurant chain, they should accept any position they are offered—perhaps in the food and beverage outlet of a large hotel or in a resort. In such cases, it will be to their advantage to accept a position as a trainee and thus begin to gain some expertise in management.

Generally, a career in restaurants requires that beginning professionals work long hours in an environment that demands fast decision-making. Hotels and resorts offer employees more manageable schedules and fewer operational difficulties. Restaurants, however, usually offer opportunities for more rapid advancement and higher salaries than lodging establishments.

Contacting Prospective Employers on Campus

The most effective way of contacting prospective employers is through the on-campus **career services** offered at most colleges and universities to assist students in finding a job. Students usually register with the career services office during their senior year. For a small registration fee or with no fee required to register, the career services office usually offers the following activities:

- Career day and graduate school fairs
- Career resource center
     Job vacancy bank
     Recruiter information
     Information on finding jobs on the Internet
     Mailing of credentials to prospective employers
     Individual career counseling and guidance
     Online listing of jobs
     Posting student resumes online
- Resume writing
- Job-interview practice

The career services office is usually in charge of sponsoring and organizing **job fairs**, a presentation where students have the opportunity of making direct contact with prospective employers. Often, the representatives of companies attending the fair are the same individuals who conduct job interviews.

If recruiters organize demonstrations or seminars on campus about their companies, students should attend and ask questions about the positions open. Students are expected to dress professionally when attending these events. Those who make a favorable first impression are more likely to be considered as potential candidates for interviewing. If the company is not interviewing at that time, students can follow up with a letter of inquiry addressed to the person they have met on campus.

Contacting Prospective Employers Directly

In addition to using a college's career services, students can directly contact hospitality corporations or individual properties to apply for a job, either by mail or e-mail. This approach is not nearly as effective as interviewing on campus because such letters usually end up lost in the steady stream of job applications received by human resources departments. The list below includes some Web sites where openings for hospitality jobs and careers can be found.

RESTAURANT MANAGEMENT

www.finediningjobs.com

www.restaurantbeast.com

www.restaurantjobs.com

www.restaurantmanager.net

HOSPITALITY/HOTELS

www.hcareers.com

www.hjo.net

www.hospitalityadventures.com

www.hospitalitycareers.net

www.hospitalitylink.com

www.hospitalitynet.nl

www.hotelcs.com

www.hoteljobsnetwork.com

www.hotelrestaurantjobs.com

www.resortjobs.com

The following list provides Internet addresses of some restaurant and lodging corporations in the United States:

Adam's Mark Hotels and Resorts	www.adamsmark.com
Best Inns and Suites	www.americasbestinns.com
Choice Hotels International	www.choicehotels.com
Country Inns and Suites	www.countryinns.com
Courtyard by Marriott	www.marriott.com/courtyard
Days Inns Worldwide	www.daysinn.com
Doubletree	www.doubletreehotels.com
Embassy Suites	www.embassysuites.com
Fairfield Inn by Marriott	www.marriott.com/fairfieldinn
Felcor Lodging Trust	www.felcor.com
Four Seasons Hotels and Resorts	www.fourseasons.com
Hilton Family	www.hiltonworldwide.com
Howard Johnson International	www.hojo.com
Hyatt Hotels Corporation	www.hyatt.com
Interstate Hotels and Resorts	www.interstatehotels.com
La Quinta	www.lq.com
Lodgian	www.lodgian.com
Loews Hotels	www.loewshotels.com
Marriott	www.marriott.com
MeriStar Hotels and Resorts	www.meristar.com
Motel 6	www.motel6.com
Omni Hotels	www.omnihotels.com
Radisson Hotels and Resorts	www.radisson.com
Ramada	www.ramada.com
Red Roof Inns	www.redroof.com
Renaissance Hotels and Resorts	www.marriott.com/renaissancehotels.com
Residence Inn by Marriott	www.marriott.com/residenceinn.com
Ritz-Carlton	www.ritzcarlton.com
Sage Hospitality Resources	www.sagehospitality.com
Sheraton	www.sheraton.com
Starwood Hotels and Resorts	www.starwoodhotels.com
Super 8 Motels	www.super8.com
Travelodge	www.travelodge.com
Wyndham Hotels and Resorts	www.wyndham.com

Many students are attracted to the hospitality industry because of its global scope. Although it is true that U.S. corporations have substantial interests overseas, including a great number of restaurants, hotels, resorts, and franchises, most of the employees in these establishments are hired locally. Occasionally, a few staff members—for example, the general manager, controller, and executive chef—may be from the United States.

The best way to work for an American company abroad is to contact its international division in the United States. Foreign corporations with headquarters overseas can also be contacted. They may be interested in graduates with a 4-year hospitality degree, particularly those who are fluent in the language spoken in that country. The following list provides the Internet addresses of some international hospitality corporations.

Accor	Worldwide	www.accor.com
AFM Hospitality Corporation	Canada	www.afmcorp.com
Atlantica Hotels International	South America	www.atlantica-hotels.com
Choice Hotels Canada	Canada	www.choicehotels.ca
Club Mediterranee SA	Worldwide	www.clubmed.com
Danubius Hotels	Hungary	www.danubiusgroup.com
Days Inn	Canada	www.daysinn.com/canada
Dorint Hotels and Resorts	Germany	www.dorint.com
Flag International Hotels	Australia and New Zealand	www.anzac.com
Golden Tulip Hotels	Holland	www.goldentulip.com
Golden Tulip Worldwide	Worldwide	www.goldentulip.com
InterContinental	Worldwide	www.interconti.com
Intercontinental Hotels Group	Worldwide	www.sixcontinentshotels.com
Jolly Hotels	Italy	www.jollyhotels.it
Kempinski Hotels and Resorts	Worldwide	www.kempinski.com
Maritim Hotels	Germany	www.maritim.com
Mercure	Worldwide	www.mercure.com
Millennium and Copthorne	Worldwide	www.millenniumhotels.com
Minotel	Switzerland	www.minotel.ch

Nikko Hotels	Japan and United States	www.nikkohotels.com
Novotel Hotel Division	Worldwide	www.novotel.com
Orbis	Poland	www.orbis.pl
Park Plaza Worldwide	Worldwide	www.parkplazaww.com
Posadas USA	Mexico and United States	www.posadas.com
Protea Hotels	South Africa	www.proteahotels.com
Ringhotels	Germany	www.ringhotels.de
Shangri-La Hotels and Resorts	Far East	www.shangri-la.com
Sofitel	Worldwide	www.sofitel.com
Sol Melia	Worldwide	www.solmelia.com
Swiss International Hotels	Worldwide	www.sih.ch
Thistle Hotels	United Kingdom	www.thistlehotels.com
Treff Hotels	Europe	www.treff-hotels.de

Students may decide to apply directly to individual properties for a position, either because they have visited a specific location or have obtained information from various sources. A short sample of the best hotels and resorts in the United States and abroad follows.

Los Angeles, CA	Bel-Air	www.belair.com
Chicago, IL	Four Seasons	www.fourseasons.com
Rome, Italy	Hassler	www.hotelhasslerroma.com
Hong Kong	Intercontinental	www.interconti.com
Dallas, TX	Mansion on Turtle Creek	www.mansiononturtlecreek.com
Phoenix/Scottsdale, AZ	Phoenician	www.thephoenician.com
Laguna Niguel, CA	Ritz-Carlton	www.ritz-carlton.com
New York	The Carlyle	www.thecarlyle.com
Sea Island, GA	The Cloister	www.cloister.com
White Sulphur Springs, WV	The Greenbrier	www.greenbrier.com
Paris, France	The Ritz	www.ritz.com
London, England	The Stafford	www.thestaffordhotel.co.uk

Students should also contact individuals they know or have met during field trips to hospitality properties, guest-speaker presentations, or industry trade shows as well as relatives, friends, and alumni working in the industry for information leading to employment.

The Perfect Resume

The **resume** is an abbreviated account of a job-seeker's education, job-related history, and qualifications. It is the primary tool that can help candidates obtain both an interview and a job. For this reason, resumes must be flawless in format, appearance, and content. In most cases, resumes should be limited to one page and should include the following components: objective, education, work experience, honors/awards, skills, extracurricular activities, and references. A **curriculum vitae** is an extensive account of an individual's experiences, but it is not appropriate for students looking for an initial job.

DANIKA JOHNSON

Current Address
Northern Arizona University
P.O. Box 3333
Flagstaff, AZ 86011
(928) 774-1711
dsj@dana.ucc.nau.edu

Permanent Address
9292 El Rey Road
Los Angeles, CA 93004
(805) 647-2231

OBJECTIVE: An entry-level position leading to management in the hospitality industry.

EDUCATION:

1999–2003	**Northern Arizona University.** Bachelor of Science in Hotel and Restaurant Management, December 2003. Cumulative GPA: 3.75.
Summer 2001	**Ecole Hoteliere Les Roches, Bluche, Switzerland.** NAU's Summer Studies in Europe Program.

INDUSTRY EXPERIENCE:

August 2001– present	**Garcia's Restaurant,** Flagstaff, Arizona *Line Cook.* Mexican and American menu specialties. Supervised the evening shift on weekends.

January 2000– May 2000	**Ritz-Carlton Hotel.** Phoenix, Arizona *Manager Trainee Internship, Rooms Division.* Was trained in front office, housekeeping, and reservations operations.
February 1997– January 1999	**The Stafford Grill.** Amarillo, Texas *Server/Hostess.* Fine-dining service. As hostess, performed restaurant closing duties when working evening shift.

HONORS/AWARDS:

Phi Eta Sigma National Honors Society

Academic scholarship from the American Hotel Foundation

NAU Dean's List, Northern Arizona University, 1999–2001

The Stafford Grill Employee of the Month Award, 1998

SKILLS: One semester of Spanish language. One semester conversational. Spanish.

EXTRACURRICULAR ACTIVITIES:

NAU Kayettes: *Corresponding Secretary,* 2000–present

Big Brothers and Sisters: Active involvement.

IFSEA: Active club member.

REFERENCES: Available upon request.

The Objective   The objective stated in a resume should provide a general idea of what a job applicant is looking for. It should be general rather than job-specific. For example, if applicants say they are looking for an entry-level management position in the hospitality industry, prospective employers will consider them for all jobs being offered. On the other hand, those applicants who write that they are looking for a position in food and beverage, for example, may be automatically disqualified for any openings in other divisions or departments. In other words, applicants should be specific only if they plan to reject any other offer that the company might offer them. Most industry professionals prefer resumes that state an objective so they can expediently find out if the candidate is willing to accept whatever position is available at the time.

Education   Job seekers should list first the hospitality degree they are about to receive, then any other relevant studies they have completed—for instance, study abroad or special certification related to the industry. If their cumulative grade point average (GPA) is substantially lower than that in their major, the latter should be listed. If the overall GPA is below average, it is advisable not to state it and to be prepared to answer questions at the time of the interview. Candidates might mention (if this is truly the case) that they have had to face a particular hardship or have had to pay their way through college by working full-time. Generally, hospitality recruiters do not put a lot of emphasis on GPA, as they understand that low marks do not necessarily mean that a candidate will not be an excellent employee. A candidate's high school GPA could be mentioned if it is notably high.

Work Experience   Recruiters will be looking closely at the work experience students have had that is related to the position they want to fill. Experience in the hospitality industry can range from answering the phones in a travel agency and working in a McDonald's to having been an employee in a five-star hotel. The most recent employment is listed first and should include dates, positions held and any experience relevant to the job, such as having supervised other employees, ordered supplies, or balanced the cash register. Internships in the industry while in college should also be listed. Students who have no industry experience should include all lab work required in courses taken—for example, in housekeeping, food and beverage, or front desk. The positions and dates of work performed must be verifiable because recruiters will most surely conduct a background check prior to hiring a candidate. Students should be prepared to answer questions about unemployed periods, about switching jobs too frequently, and about the reasons for leaving a position.

Honors/Awards   Academic honors, scholarships, and awards received in the workplace should be stated, such as Dean's List, student of the year, employee of the month, and so on. Employers will be looking for scholarly and work-related signs of leadership.

Skills   Special abilities—for example, knowledge of another language, extraordinary culinary ability, or exceptional experience with technological systems—should be listed.

Extracurricular Activities   Some hospitality companies do look for activities beyond education and industry work experience. Involvement in public and social activities is seen as a sign that the candidate will be willing to contribute to the social fabric of the community where the place of work is located. Membership in academic clubs, such as the National Society for Minorities in Hospitality, and community organizations, such as Big Brothers and Big Sisters, should be listed.

References   Because the main purpose of submitting a resume is to be invited for an interview, a **list of references** does not serve an immediate purpose. Stating that references are "available upon request" is sufficient. However, students should have such a list prepared in advance. They should ask permission from academic instructors and industry managers they know well to use them as references and have a typed list ready to be given to prospective employers upon request. Three or four individuals who know the student well should suffice. The sample reference list below includes two professors and two industry supervisors.

REFERENCES

Danika Johnson

Matt A. Casado
Professor
School of Hotel and Restaurant Management
Northern Arizona University
P.O. Box 5638
Flagstaff, AZ 86011
Telephone: (928) 523-1712
E-mail: *matt.casado@nau.edu*

Peter Fletcher
Lecturer
Hospitality Management
Tidewater Community College
1700 College Crescent
Virginia Beach, VA 23456
Telephone: (757) 321-7173
E-mail: *ptchef@tc.cc.va*

Eric W. Rande
Front Office Manager
Hyatt Regency at Macy's Plaza
711 South Hope Street
Los Angeles, CA 90017
Telephone: (213) 629-3230
E-mail: *Erande@laxrlpo.hyatt.com*

Anne P. James
Franchise Service Director
Choice Hotels International
23425 N. 39th Drive, Suite 104
Glendale, AZ 85310
Telephone: (623) 516-2980
E-mail: *apgodi@choicehotels.com*

SITUATION 1.1   Preparing a Resume

Melanie S. Olson is taking her senior seminar class at Colorado State University, Fort Collins. She plans to graduate in May 2005, and her objective is to find a position with a hospitality company, preferably in the rooms division of a large golf resort. She attended Denver Community College during the fall semester of 2002. She was an exchange student at Sheffield College, England, during the spring semester of 2004. Her cumulative GPA is 2.8 and her major GPA is 3.76.

Melanie's work experience is as follows: desk clerk from 6/15/04 to the present at Rodeway Inn, Denver; assistant manager from 9/5/03 to 12/31/04, at Woodlands Inn Bed and Breakfast, Boulder; and line cook at Mecca Grill Restaurant, Aurora, Colorado, from 2/2/2000 to 5/12/2000. She has received the following honors/awards: Mortar Board Senior Honor Society, 2002, Eta Sigma Delta Honor Society, 2002/2003, and HRM Dean's List, spring 2004. Melanie understands and speaks Spanish quite well and knows how to operate a copying machine.

She has been a member of the Hospitality Entrepreneurs Club in college and has been active in the Denver Cancer Society League. Two professors at CSU, one instructor at DCC and the Rodeway Inn manager in Denver have agreed to serve as references for her.

ASSIGNMENT: Compile a resume with the information given.

The Cover Letter

When resumes are sent to companies, they must be accompanied by a **cover letter** whose content and format must, like the resume, be correctly done. An example of a cover letter is shown below. If possible, the letter should be addressed to the person responsible for screening or hiring. The body of the letter should be divided into three parts: (1) a clear statement of the purpose of the letter; (2) a brief explanation of the reasons why the company should be interested in hiring you (here, you should highlight any industry experience, as well as personal traits and professional skills related to the job in question) and (3) a restatement of your desire to work for the company. All statements should be honest and truthful. The cover letter should match the typeface used on the resume. All correspondence sent through regular mail should be typed on at least medium-grade paper.

Colorado State University
P.O. Box 3333
Fort Collins, CO 80523
(303) 774-1711
mso4@dana.ucc.csu.edu

October 19, 2005

Ms. Meghan O'Connor
General Manager
Arizona Biltmore Resort and Spa
2400 East Missouri
Phoenix, AZ 85016

Dear Ms. O'Connor:

I recently had the opportunity to visit your resort while in the Phoenix area. I was so impressed by the beautiful facilities and the excellent service you offer your guests that I thought it would be an exciting experience to work for a company such as yours.

I will be graduating from the School of Hotel and Restaurant Management at Northern Arizona University in December of this year. Over the past four years, I have been exposed to the hospitality industry through academic courses and projects and through work experience. I am now seeking to gain comprehensive knowledge about the industry by joining a company that offers a good management-training program. My excellent work ethic and desire to excel would make me an asset to your establishment.

I have enclosed my resume for your consideration. I would be happy to interview with you about employment opportunities in your resort at any time. I look forward to hearing from you.

Sincerely,

Melanie Olson

Enc.

SITUATION 1.2   Preparing a Cover Letter

ASSIGNMENT: Compile a cover letter to accompany your application based on your own resume.

Learning About a Company

Before interviewing, students should research the background of the company they hope to join. This preparation will help candidates answer questions asked by the interviewer, such as "What do you know about us?" It can also help them make comments indicating that they have made the effort to be prepared, such as "I understand that your company has opened six units in California in the last 3 years. How are they doing?" Information about corporations can be obtained at their Web sites or at the library. The annual reports of publicly held companies, filed with the Securities and Exchange Commission, provide detailed financial information. The records and performance of privately held companies can be found in reports published by trade magazines such as *Restaurants and Institutions*. Calling or visiting with people already working at a specific property can also provide students with a personal perspective of a company's operations and management philosophy.

The Interview

Countless books have been written about job interviewing, but the basic points to remember are these: Be on time, show a positive attitude, and be professionally attired. Most executives at hospitality companies interact with other professionals and guests dressed in business attire and they thus expect to see job candidates dressed in a similar fashion.

At the time of the interview, it is important to remember that the persons you will be interviewing with are there to recruit promising new employees for their companies; that is, these companies need you as much as you need them. Your goal should be to sell yourself, to make it clear that you are eager to learn about the industry and have a commitment to work hard. You should answer questions honestly, clearly, and concisely, without trying to dominate the conversation. Most interviews involve four types of questions:

- *Direct:* A **direct question** is one that usually begins with *what, when, where, who,* or *why*.
- *Open-ended:* An **open-ended question** leaves the answer entirely to you.
- *Leading:* A question that is usually answered with *yes* or *no* is a **leading question**.
- *Situational:* A **situational question** asks about a hypothetical situation.

The following questions might be asked on a first interview:

What do you know about our company?

Why should we hire you?

In what ways do you think you can make a contribution to our company?

Why did you choose hospitality as a career?

What do you see yourself doing 3 years from now?

What motivates you to put forth your best effort?

Which is most important to you, the type of job we are offering or the salary?

Do you have plans for continued study?

What have you learned from the mistakes you made in the past?

In what kind of work environment will you be most comfortable?

Are you willing to travel?

Are you willing to be transferred often?

Why did you decide to seek a position with this company?

What are the most important rewards you expect in a hospitality career?

What are your long-range career objectives?

Will you relocate when necessary?

What qualifications should a successful manager possess?

How much do you expect to be earning in 5 years?

What do you consider to be your greatest strengths and weaknesses?

How do you determine success?

You should be able to answer each of these questions concisely and intelligently. The career services office in most colleges provides help in interviewing techniques. Candidates should be ready to answer questions about industry-specific situations—(for instance, "What do you understand about yield management in hotels?") personal questions ("Would you mind being transferred to a location back east after your training period?") and behavior-based questions ("Do you work well under pressure?") Conversely, candidates should be prepared to ask the interviewer questions. Asking pertinent questions about the company—for example, "Can you describe the training-program you offer to first-time hires?"—will convey the impression that you are a serious candidate. On the other hand, asking too many questions at the time of the first interview is counterproductive, as it might portray you as being overanxious.

You should not address interviewers by their first names unless you are invited to do so as the interview progresses. Extra materials, such as a list of references, letters of recommendation or awards, and academic transcripts should be brought to the interview. After the interview, send a thank-you note to the interviewer, expressing again your desire to join the company.

Criteria for Hiring

The criteria for hiring a new employee vary from company to company. In general, recruiters will rank skills as follows:

1. Verbal communication (ability to speak in a fluent, concise manner)
2. Work experience in industry, internships, labs
3. Personal appearance (professional attire and demeanor)
4. Knowledge and enthusiasm about the company
5. Extracurricular involvement in community and college organizations
6. Grade point average (not critical to hospitality companies)

The ranking shows that interviewers will judge you first on the way you communicate. If you have difficulty in expressing your thoughts clearly and concisely, you should practice with a career services expert or with a friend until you develop fluency in your answering patterns. A high GPA is not considered vital by most companies as it is generally accepted that there is little correlation between grades and future performance in the workplace.

Second Interviews

It is common for companies interested in hiring job candidates to invite them to a second interview at corporate headquarters. Being invited to such an interview indicates that the company is seriously considering hiring you. Usually, the company will pay for your transportation and lodging. In some cases, several staff members will interview you, asking general questions and observing your reactions to questions on specific industry situations. Some companies will ask you to spend one day on the job—for instance, preparing food in the kitchen or serving in the dining room. At this time, everything you do will be evaluated. Your behavior will also be observed in informal settings—for example, while having lunch or during dinner.

Interview Follow-up

Remember to follow up all interviews and contacts made with prospective employers with a thank-you note or telephone call. After the initial interview, a written note thanking recruiters for their time and stressing a desire to work for the company can be effective. In some cases, you may get a job offer while still being considered by another company. After an appropriate period of time, you can call to ask if a decision has been made.

ACCEPTING THE JOB OFFER

If you are lucky enough to receive multiple offers of employment, you should evaluate them carefully before making a final selection. The critical question you must consider for any offer is whether the position will fit your values, interests, and overall career goals. Issues such as location, title of the position, salary, benefits, moving expenses, housing availability, and opportunity for advancement should also be considered very carefully. Often, employees already working with the company can provide valuable information.

You should also keep in mind the type of company making the offer, **Independently owned companies** may offer a limited career scope if the number of properties they operate is small. On occasion, these companies belong to local individuals who intend to speculate on the real estate value of the establishments. It is common that independent owners franchise their properties from a national chain. You should also understand that being hired by a **franchised property** does not mean that you will be working for the corporation holding the brand name; that is, being an employee of a Holiday Inn resort owned by a local doctor does not mean that you will be working for the Holiday Inn Corporation. Generally, a **multi-unit chain** operating under the direct control of the chain's headquarters will offer you the best opportunities to advance in your career. Usually, an employee who has been trained and has worked in a supervisory position for a large hotel chain is promoted to a management job after a reasonable amount of time. Opportunities for advancement with **management companies** also depend on the number of units the companies operate, as some of them have many properties, and others just a few units.

When you decide to accept an offer, you should request a signed contract or, at least, a signed letter confirming the initial position, salary, benefits and payment of expenses associated with the hiring.

Sometimes a company may want to test your ability working as an hourly employee before placing you on a management-training track. In such a case, you should obtain a firm commitment from the company that the job will lead to a management-track position within a reasonable period of time. Accepting an hourly position—say, as a front desk clerk—without a clear opportunity for advancement should be the last resort for a graduate of a 4-year baccalaureate program. Situation 1.3 lists three job offers made to a hotel and restaurant management senior after interviewing on campus.

SITUATION 1.3   Accepting a Job Offer

After several interviews with hotel and restaurant management companies on campus, you are offered three positions: The first is with a management company, based in Denver, that currently manages 75 lodging properties, all franchised. The second offer is from the Marriott Corporation of Salt Lake City, and the third is from Brinker International of San Antonio.

1. The job offer is a position as an assistant to the coffee shop manager of a 350-room Radisson-franchised hotel owned by a local insurance company in Denver, Colorado. You have been told that the management company for which you are interviewing is going to need several food and beverage (F&B) managers for new hotels being acquired next year. The company, which operates 75 properties in the United States and one in the Bahamas, offers a 6-month management training period in which the employee will have to perform frontline work in the F&B department, housekeeping, and front desk. Promotion after the initial training is not guaranteed. The initial job pays $23,500 annually and includes medical and dental insurance. No participation in a retirement program is provided until employees reach department-manager status. The company does not offer a relocation stipend.

2. The job offer from Marriott is a manager-in-training position as assistant in the housekeeping department of a Residence Inn in Salt Lake

City, Utah. You have been told that you will be trained directly by the executive housekeeper who has been with the property for 10 years. The salary guaranteed for the first year is $22,000. Full dental and medical insurance is covered by the company. A limited retirement plan is offered to new management-track employees. The company will pay $1,500 for moving expenses to Salt Lake and will provide housing in an apartment building near the hotel at $400 per month.

3. The third offer involves participation in an intensive training program at a Chili's Restaurant in San Antonio, Texas. The program is very well structured. The candidate will work the floor, the kitchen, and the cash register for 6 months before being promoted to unit assistant manager. The company, you have been told, is expanding very fast. A friend working for Brinker International has told you that the company is excellent and that restaurant general managers in some locations are making more than $100,000 per year. This particular unit, which is located near the airport, does not provide an insurance or retirement plan until the first promotion. The starting salary is $33,000 annually and the company will pay all moving expenses to San Antonio.

ASSIGNMENT: Discuss the advantages and disadvantages of accepting each of the three positions offered.

CLASS ASSIGNMENT: Students will compile their own resume and a list of references, together with the cover letter prepared in Situation 1.2, applying for a management-trainee position addressed to an imaginary company. After the instructor has reviewed the last draft, students should prepare a final version of the three documents, typed in 12-point font on standard-size quality paper. Headings should be typed in bold and in roman typeface, not in italics.

KEY CONCEPTS/TERMS

career services

cover letter

curriculum vitae

direct question

franchised property

independently owned company

job fair

leading question

list of references

management company

multi-unit chain

open-ended question

resume

situational question

Chapter 2

Food Operations

CHAPTER OBJECTIVES

- Learn about problem-solving strategies in food outlets of lodging operations.
- Review the characteristics of food service in institutional operations.
- Discuss distinctive aspects of restaurant operations.
- Resolve situational cases of food service operations.

OVERVIEW

This chapter describes the different characteristics of food service in lodging establishments, and institutional, and restaurant operations. Lodging establishments generally operate four distinct types of food outlets, each with its own production and service characteristics: (1) coffee shops, which provide casual service in a relaxed atmosphere; (2) fine-dining restaurants, which offer elaborate menus and impeccable service; (3) banquet departments, which specialize in producing and serving several functions simultaneously, and (4) room service, which usually fill orders to guest rooms that may be far away from the service centers where meals are prepared and set up. Institutional food services must face the challenge of feeding a huge number of customers, in university, school, and factory settings. Individual restaurants face, in most cases, the challenge of operating in a competitive environment while having to manage a diverse, often unreliable, workforce. This chapter offers several situational cases that will help prepare students for operations in these food-industry segments.

After the management-training period, which may last between 3 months and 1 year, new employees in the food service industry are usually offered positions as supervisors or assistant managers in one of the following segments:

***Lodging:** Coffee shops, restaurants, room service, banquets.*
***Restaurants:** Fine dining, family dining, quick service (fast food).*
***Institutional:** Cafeterias in factories, school districts and universities, and club operations.*

FOOD SERVICE IN LODGING OPERATIONS

Working in food service in lodging operations is a necessary step for graduates to acquire the required expertise to become general managers in lodging establishments. Most initial jobs offered by recruiting companies are in food service operations. Recruited students are assigned to a food outlet in a hotel or resort during their management-training period, after which they are generally promoted to positions as supervisors or assistant managers in the establishment where they have trained or they are transferred to a different property. Lodging operations are visited by a diverse clientele, ranging from politicians and foreign diplomats to business travelers and families from around the world. The scope of operations of food service in these types of establishments are broad and fast-paced. A typical scenario might follow this pattern: A large number of customers is expecting to be served breakfast in a short period of time, both in the coffee shop and by room service, while a large breakfast banquet is taking place simultaneously in one of the hotel's meeting rooms. At lunch, guests and businesspeople from the local community linger over a 1-hour, three-course meal in the dining room. In the evening, the pace is generally more leisurely but guests expect to be served elaborate meals with impeccable service. In some establishments, these varied services throughout the day are provided from the property's only kitchen, making the operation very complex indeed.

As students learn early in their college career, there are several categories of lodging properties, ranging from 5-star hotels and resorts to unpretentious motels along the highway. In all cases, guests have certain expectations about the food they order. They want it to be served hot (when it is a hot dish), attractively garnished, and delicious in taste. The waitperson is expected to be attentive to details, efficient, and courteous. In all of the services provided, staff members must maintain an optimum level of quality at all times, a difficult goal to achieve given that the food industry is notorious for very high employee turnover. Nevertheless, food service is an exciting aspect of the hospitality industry. In some locations, it carries with it a lot of unforgettable glamour. For example, I was the maˆtre d'hôtel at the Royal Court Hotel in Chelsea at the time the Beatles stayed regularly at the property and had their meals in the restaurant. It can happen to anyone working in the hospitality industry, a perk not available in most professions.

Food Service in Coffee Shops of Lodging Operations

Coffee shops in lodging properties can be described as restaurants with simplified menus where guests can take a light meal at most hours of the day. Most coffee shops in hotels and resorts are designed to serve breakfast in a short period of time (usually between 7 and 9 AM). The reason is that guests, particularly on weekdays, need to check out early to continue their travels by road, plane, or train, or to keep business appointments. For this reason, breakfast is fast-paced for both kitchen and service personnel.

Although not as hectic in pace, lunch must also be provided rapidly as most people have only one hour to eat a meal before going back to work. As a result, the menu in coffee shops should be uncomplicated and easy to prepare, particularly if the menu items are prepared **à la minute** (as they are ordered). The most common complaints made by guests in coffee shops during breakfast and, to a lesser extent, lunch, are long waits to be seated, excessive time before they are greeted by servers and given the menu, slow kitchen service, and unreasonable time waiting to get the check. Service during breakfast and lunch can be slowed considerably if there are not enough buspersons to clear and reset the tables. New employees recruited to work in this type of setting, particularly during breakfast service, must strive to provide speedy, efficient service to their guests. The situation changes at dinnertime, when guests usually have more time to enjoy their meal. As a matter of fact, most people do not like to be rushed during dinner and prefer service that is attentive but not hasty. Situation 2.1 deals with problems often found in coffee shop operations.

SITUATION 2.1   Problem-solving in Coffee Shop Operations

After a period of 6 months as a manager-trainee at a hotel in downtown Phoenix, Niki Butler has been promoted to the position of manager of a coffee shop in a 4-star business hotel owned by the same company. Located at the airport of a large city in New England, the coffee shop has been having serious difficulties since the manager Niki is replacing was promoted to food and beverage director at another out-of-state property. The corporate human resources director has confided to Niki that a major overhaul of the coffee shop may be necessary. Niki hopes that the hospitality courses that she has taken in college and the experience gained in Phoenix as a manager-trainee have qualified her as a potential problem-solver. Soon after arriving at the property, Niki gathered information from the hotel's general manager and the acting coffee shop manager as well as from some employees. She also read comment cards (most of them complaints) filed in the F&B office. Four major sources of problems were identified:

1. Breakfast service was very slow. Several comments explicitly stated that it took almost 50 minutes from the time the guests arrived in the coffee shop to the time they left.
2. During most peak hours (between 7:30 and 9:00 AM on weekdays) a line of guests waiting to be seated formed at the hostess desk. The average waiting time was 5 minutes.
3. Although orders in the kitchen were processed quickly, the food often got cold before it was brought to the customer's table.
4. On many days several breakfast charges were not posted to guests' folios before the actual checkout took place. Niki observed that the host/cashier was often busy cleaning tables while the checks piled up

by the computer monitor. The front office manager has complained to the general manager that the late charges cause excess work as breakfast charges have to be billed separately to guests' credit card numbers after they have departed from the hotel. In the case of cash-only guests, the revenue is lost.

ASSIGNMENT: Propose the necessary steps needed to improve the situation in the coffee shop. Be specific about the time waiting in line, the slow service, the food being served cold, and the delayed posting of guest charges.

Food Service in Restaurants of Lodging Operations

In addition to casual dining outlets such as coffee shops, lodging properties usually have upscale or family restaurants to cater to their guests' dining needs. The quality of most restaurants is linked to the category of the establishment, although this is not always the case; there may be fancy hotels and resorts that offer mediocre menus and service, and modest properties with first-class food menus and service.

In general, family restaurants are midscale outlets where guests can enjoy familiar foods that are reasonably priced. Casual dress is usually acceptable. Most family restaurants offer a modified **table d'hôte menu**—a single-priced series of dishes served as a whole meal—with a good selection of items that are offered **à la carte**—listed and priced separately. Children's menus in this type of restaurant are a must.

Fine dining restaurants generally offer a choice of sophisticated dishes prepared after **French cuisine**—a cooking style featuring the traditional dishes and cooking methods of France—or from **nouvelle cuisine**—a modern cooking style featuring new ingredients. The service in signature restaurants is elaborate, and servers are elegantly dressed. In the best restaurants in Europe, especially in the United Kingdom, head waiters are clad in tail coats and starched white shirts. It is a must that the menu in upscale restaurants be complemented with a complete list of first-class vintage wines, both domestic and imported. It is common to have a **sommelier**—the person serving as a wine steward—recommend the appropriate wine for the dishes to be served. Often, some of the dishes are carved or prepared tableside, sometimes flamed by a specialist—by the **dining room captain** in the United States, the **chef de rang** in Europe.

Employees hired to work in restaurants of lodging properties must adapt to the type of service offered. While the service approach in midscale or family restaurants is casual, relaxed, and familiar, fine dining operations require a formal, sophisticated demeanor (bordering on the theatrical) on the part of the floor crew. Because of the cost of specialized labor and the elaborate composition of menus in upscale food outlets, the profit from food sales is usually low, with a food cost of around 40 percent of food revenue. However, the bottom line can be positively improved with the sale of expensive vintage wines, aperitifs, and liqueurs.

SITUATION 2.2   Menu Knowledge of Upscale Restaurant Managers

After two years in the industry, John Moreo, a graduate of a 4-year hospitality program, accepts a job offer with a five-star hotel in New York City as assistant manager of the Peacock Terrace Restaurant. On one of the manager's days off, John is in charge of making arrangements for a dinner being hosted by Victoria Welch, a prominent, affluent visitor from Oklahoma who is staying in one of the hotel's luxury suites. Mrs. Welch wants to entertain a group of friends at the restaurant and has reserved a quiet table for twelve. A world-traveled friend of Mrs. Welch has suggested that the following set menu be served:

Crème Dubarry

✳

Fillet of Sole Véronique

✳

Grilled Tournedos Choron
Château Potatoes
Panaché de Légumes

✳

Cherries Jubilée

Mrs. Welch is not familiar with French cuisine terminology and would like to know more about the dishes her friend has recommended. She asks John to explain to her in detail the preparation and composition of the dishes. John immediately tries to come up with a coherent, professional answer.

He recalls several facts learned in school. Soups are categorized within three groups: clear, naturally thickened **(potage)**, and thickened with **roux** or **beurre manié**. John also remembers that **Dubarry** means that the main ingredient in the soup is a vegetable, but he doesn't recall which one. He knows what a **fillet** of fish is but he doesn't remember what method of cooking is usually used for this particular dish. Is the fish baked, fried, grilled, poached, or **en papillote**? And what does **Véronique** mean? It must be an ingredient used in the sauce with which the sole is **napped**. And, what type of sauce could it be?

What about the **entrée**? He has a feeling that the meat is beef and that **tournedos** is a type of cut. What does tournedos mean? And **choron**? John is sure that it is not a type of garnish but a sauce. John remembers that there are five basic sauces: **béchamel**, **velouté**, **espagnole**, **tomato**, and **hollandaise/**

béarnaise. How could he describe sauce choron to Mrs. Welch? And the dish **garniture**? How are **château potatoes** prepared, and what does **panaché de légumes** consist of?

John does, however, remember very clearly all about **cherries jubilée**; he even recalls that this dessert was first prepared in honor of British Queen Victoria and Prince Albert in the nineteenth century. The dessert is prepared tableside by heating the bing cherries in their juice, adding preheated **kirschwasser**, a liqueur that is used to flame the mixture, that is then poured on mounds of vanilla ice cream.

ASSIGNMENT: Help John Moreo describe in detail the remaining menu dishes to Mrs. Welch.

Room Service in Lodging Operations

Food and beverage service to guest rooms in lodging operations is offered by all luxury hotels 24 hours a day. Most 4-star business hotels provide room service from 6 AM to about 12 AM, delegating the work to the bell staff from midnight to 6 AM. Some upscale properties provide **butler service**—personalized service intended to provide all F&B guest needs plus other requests, such as shirt pressing or delivery of specialized newspapers or magazines.

Although few guests order room service at lunchtime, a large number of orders are placed at breakfast. Because of the intensity of the demand in a short period of time (usually between 7 and 8 AM weekdays), room service is a very difficult outlet to manage. The room service staff must have a good **mise en place**—the preparation of foods and equipment before orders begin to come in. Typically, properties without adequate space for many trays and service carts set up in advance face serious problems delivering breakfast to the rooms on time; in such settings, portable shelving racks can help. Some large hotels have service stations on each floor or on every other one where servers assemble and coordinate the orders. Food is often sent to these stations by way of a **dumbwaiter**—a small elevator used to send food and equipment to upper floors. Some properties use service elevators equipped with crockery, silverware, juices, dry goods and beverage-making equipment so continental breakfast can quickly be prepared while on the way to the floor. To prevent misunderstanding by guests, a note on the room service menu and breakfast door tags should state that it may take up to 20 minutes to deliver an order. However, if guests are told this, they will become irate if it takes more than half an hour to receive their breakfasts.

Dinners served through room service in upscale properties are expected to be elegant affairs. Service carts are usually equipped with a food warmer cabinet or **rechaud**—a small heated stand where finished dishes are kept warm. Establishments using trays instead of carts must provide fast delivery service so that hot dishes reach guests at the right temperature.

Because of the need to serve a large number of orders simultaneously, room service personnel must be very well trained and a sufficient number of them scheduled to provide efficient service. Many phone orders must also be taken in short periods of time. The expeditor must take orders carefully to avoid extra requests by guests after the food has been received. For example, if a guest orders prime rib, the order taker should ask if he or she would like any condiment such as horseradish or sauce. A guest requesting horseradish *after* the order has been delivered will cause a server to make a second trip, wasting precious time.

Room service managers must control labor expenses carefully, balancing the staffing of the department so that labor cost percentages are not exceedingly high while maintaining the quality of service. Upselling by order takers is a priority in a department where the productivity ratios are traditionally low. For example, a bottle of wine sold with a prime rib order will substantially improve the check total.

Graduates accepting a position in room service must be good service and labor organizers and have sufficient physical stamina to serve an area that is several times larger than the property's restaurants. Situation 2.3 illustrates how effective scheduling can affect labor cost in room service operations.

SITUATION 2.3   Room Service Labor Cost Control

Eileen Hill was hired by the Hyatt Corporation to be trained as manager-trainee for 5 months in a busy hotel in Chicago. The establishment was steadily patronized by business travelers on weekdays and by families and tourists on weekends. As a result, the occupancy of the hotel was around 78 percent throughout the year. After her management-training period, Eileen was offered the position of room service manager at an annual salary of $32,000. She gladly accepted.

During her first interview with the director of food and beverage, Eileen was given a synopsis of the room service operation and was asked to focus on the resolution of existing problems. Basically, the department was running well; however, the labor cost was exceedingly high. The F&B director told Eileen that he hoped the percentage would be lowered by about 5 percent without negatively affecting the quality of service. In addition, the director also expected to lower the number of complaints by guests that he received regularly for slow delivery during peak breakfast hours.

On taking over the department, Eileen observed that, although orders for hot dishes were filled promptly by the kitchen, the four room service waiters on duty were not sufficient to cope with the orders in a reasonable period of time. The daily standing schedule for the department (seven days a week) was as follows:

Current Room Service Standing Work Schedule	
Server 1	6 AM–2 PM
Server 2	6 AM–2 PM
Server 3	7 AM–10 AM
Server 4	7 AM–10 AM
Server 5	2 PM–10 PM
Server 6	4 PM–midnight
Order-taker 1	6 AM–2 PM
Order-taker 2	2 PM–10 PM

The budgeted room service F&B revenue for the year was set at $459,000. The average hourly wage is $4.75 for servers and $6.55 for order takers. Eileen worked out the annual labor cost of the department, including the manager's $32,000 salary.

In order to cut down costs, she modified the standing schedule as follows:

New Room Service Standing Work Schedule	
Server 1	6 AM–2 PM
Server 2	7 AM–10 AM
Server 3	7 AM–10 AM
Server 4	7 AM–10 AM
Server 5	2 PM–10 PM
Server 6	4 PM–midnight
Order-taker 1	6 AM–2 PM

Her rationale for the changes was (1) to reinforce service between breakfast peak hours to eliminate complaints and (2) to lower the current labor cost. She also asked for two mobile racks to increase tray mise en place space. The phone answering service was modified so that calls between 2 PM and midnight would be forwarded to the coffee shop hostess station (open 24 hours), arranging for orders to be taken there if the room service staff was away from the phone. Eileen also intended to cover the phones as much as her managerial duties allowed.

ASSIGNMENT: Work out the annual labor cost percentage for the two schedules based on the yearly revenue of $459,000 and find out the difference in percentage points. Comment on Eileen's proposed changes in the department. (Do not include employee-related labor cost expenses.) What else do you think could be done to improve operations?

Banquets in Lodging Operations

The coordination of food service in coffee shops, restaurants, and room service outlets in lodging operations is relatively easy when compared with that of banquets, particularly if the hotel or resort specializes in large conventions and functions. For example, it is not uncommon for a hotel to be serving several banquets for hundreds of people concurrently—along with a wedding reception and a gala charity ball. The coordination of these simultaneous events could be compared with a military battle plan in which the sales office, the executive chef, and the catering director act as commanders of their respective forces in a coordinated effort to achieve victory. Manager-trainees joining the banquets/catering department of a large lodging establishment can be guaranteed that they will never have a dull moment while on duty.

Food service in the catering department becomes complex when the property has only one kitchen to service multiple outlets. Large operations have a **banquet kitchen**—a separate kitchen where meals for large functions are prepared and assembled. Banquet service can be performed by plating the food in the kitchen and carrying the dishes on trays to the tables or by serving the food directly from large oval dishes onto the guests' plates. The second system is traditional in Europe and requires specialized servers who are skilled in serving food with a fork and a spoon held in one hand while holding the platter with the other. A second server then passes the garnish and a third does the same with the gravy (if this is required).

Usually, the banquet set-up crew is drawn from full-time employees while most of the servers are part-time or on-call workers. It should be a priority for the catering department to identify servers who are willing to work on-call in order to keep a low labor cost. Generally, retired or semiretired experienced workers can be found who prefer to work on a part-time basis. The menus offered for catering functions can range from the simple (a luncheon for the local Rotary Club) to the extraordinary (a five-course ethnic food banquet honoring a distinguished foreign dignitary). In all cases, the catering department must obtain adequate labor and food costs. The food cost percentage for most banquet functions should range between 25 and 30 percent of the cover price charged.

Employees joining the catering department of busy lodging operations must have an excellent sense of organization and enough stamina to cope with the fast pace typical of this department. They will find that successfully meeting the challenge of serving large numbers of people can be demanding but exhilarating. Situation 2.4 is an exercise on menu pricing inherent in banquet planning.

SITUATION 2.4   Costing a Banquet Menu

J.R. Howey, a graduate from Penn State University's hotel and restaurant management program, has been promoted to assistant catering manager at a golf resort and spa in Florida. His boss has delegated to him the job of costing a customer-written dinner menu for a regular guest, the manager of one of the Nissan car dealerships in the Miami area. After agreeing on the menu, J.R.

requested a portion cost sheet from the resort's F&B controller who came up with the following cost of food:

Cup of vichyssoise	$1.35
Mimosa salad	0.70
Grilled filet mignon (12 oz.)	4.80
Duchesse potatoes	0.33
Vegetable bouquetière	1.48
Sauce périgourdine	0.52
Benedictine iced biscuit	1.13
Rolls and butter	0.56
Coffee	0.18

J.R. applied the markup for a food cost percentage of 28 and faxed the proposal to the Nissan customer. The next morning J.R. received a call from the car dealer who found the cost per person a touch high. He asked J.R. to provide him with a lower price after reducing the size of the filet mignon from 12 ounces to 8. He also asked to have the quote right away as he was about to go on a business trip and wanted to decide on the dinner before leaving for the airport. Not wanting to lose this business, J.R. decided not only to lower the price per person by adjusting the size and cost of the filet mignon but also to increase the food cost by 2 percent.

ASSIGNMENT: Work out the new price per person for this dinner.

INSTITUTIONAL FOOD SERVICE

Several hospitality corporations that recruit graduating seniors from hospitality management programs are in the business of providing food service to institutions, such as colleges and universities, hospitals, manufacturing companies, national parks, and school districts. Aramark, Sodexho-Marriott, and Compass Group are among the corporations that specialize in institutional food service. Often, these companies contract the food services to be provided to institutions for a specified number of years.

In most cases, food is prepared in large quantities and served cafeteria style; that is, cold and hot items are displayed in refrigerated or heated counters fitted with serving trays from which diners select their choices as they move along the line. One advantage of this system is that labor cost is minimized because servers are not needed. Marketing dollars are also eliminated because the clientele is usually a captive audience having limited or no choice because of the location of the institutions. College students, for instance, generally find it more convenient to dine on campus than having to drive to a restaurant in town. In school districts and hospitals, the competition is nonexistent.

Graduates accepting job offers from institutional food service companies usually find that their duties are less demanding than if they worked for lodging or restaurant companies because they do not have to worry much about where to find and how to keep customers. Meals at institutions are also predictable in number of covers because customers usually buy meal plans they must use up, as is the case in universities, or they get discounted prices when food is subsidized by the institution for which they work, as in worker cafeterias. Another advantage to working for institutional food services in colleges and universities is that an ample labor pool of inexpensive workers is available. Foreign students that are not allowed to work in private sector establishments can do so within the university campus. On the other hand, managers of institutional food service must be familiar with special aspects of food preparation. For instance, employees working in hospitals or nursing homes must be proficient in dietetics, and those working in school districts must know about all aspects of nutrition.

Sanitation is an important aspect of institutional food service because of the complexity of the cooking equipment needed for large-scale food preparation and holding for extended periods of time. Keeping the hot and cold food dishes at the right temperature can be a challenge to management. Situation 2.5 deals with a dilemma that commercial-food-preparation managers may encounter in institutional operations.

SITUATION 2.5   Cost Analysis

After graduating from a 4-year hospitality management program, you are hired by a contract management company providing institutional food service to a large school district in Illinois. The **cycle menu**—a series of menus that rotates over a period of time—requires that a large number of potatoes be mashed, baked or used for French fries and salad. Last year, a total of 9,758 pounds of potatoes was processed. The company has been using pre-peeled potatoes purchased in 24-pound bags. Given the large amount of potatoes used, your boss wonders if the company could save some money by having the potatoes peeled on premises. She asks you to explore that possibility by conducting a cost-comparison study. You decide to look into the matter and contact the purchasing agent and the controller who provide you with the following information:

- Pre-peeled potatoes are currently purchased in 24-pound bags for $21.32 each.
- Unpeeled potatoes are sold in 50-pound boxes for $13.45 each.
- Peeling and eyeing time for a box of potatoes is 40 minutes average.
- The hourly wage paid to a potato peeler is $6.95 an hour.
- Payroll taxes and employee benefits are 27 percent of hourly wage.
- Peeling loss average is 15 percent.

ASSIGNMENT: Based on the 9,758 pounds of potatoes used last year, find the dollars that could be saved annually by selecting the most cost-saving method.

RESTAURANT FOOD SERVICE

The career objective of many hotel and restaurant management graduates is to work in restaurants; some are attracted by the opportunity of substantial starting salaries and the opportunity for fast advancement, others by the excitement of working in a dynamic, fast-paced atmosphere. Some students may want to gain experience in the restaurant business to eventually open their own establishments. As with lodging properties, restaurants can be chain-owned or franchised to an individual or to operating companies.

Most restaurant-recruiting in colleges and universities is done by chains that specialize in **casual dining**—relaxed food service offered by restaurants such as Red Lobster and Ruby Tuesday; **family restaurants**, such as Perkins and Sizzler which offer dishes that appeal to families; **ethnic restaurants**, such as El Torito (Mexican) and Benihana (Japanese); and **quick service restaurants**, which specialize in serving (almost instantly) burgers (McDonald's), pizza (Domino's), seafood (Long John Silver's), chicken (KFC), and sandwiches (Subway). Most of the restaurant chains recruiting on campus have well-designed management-training programs for their new recruits. Usually, graduates are required to work the kitchen, the floor, and the cashier desk before they are given supervisory duties. The expansion of some restaurant chains can be so swift that some hotel and restaurant management graduates are given positions as general managers in very short periods of time. In some cases, enterprising individuals have reached regional management jobs within 5 years of being hired. Compensation in these positions, requiring the coordination of several units, includes six-figure salaries, generous benefits, and other perks.

One of the drawbacks of working in restaurants is the difficulty of keeping a dedicated workforce. In some cases, turnover in the lower ranks can reach very high percentages as workers leave in search of better jobs. This and the implacable industry competition can often lead to management burnout. In addition, the income margin for such restaurants can be very low—often, as little as 10 cents of every revenue dollar of the food revenue. In most cases, adequate profit is generated by serving large numbers of meals. This requires that managers be extremely cost conscious in the control of labor and food expenses. Factors such as excessive portion sizes, overproduction, inefficient purchasing and receiving, excessive spoilage, improper use of leftovers, and pilferage can cause the restaurant to fail. For example, if one order of roast beef calls for 9 ounces of meat and the cost to serve 1 ounce is 28 cents, every time the order is overportioned by 1 ounce the restaurant will lose 28 cents. If the restaurant serves an average of 80 orders of roast beef a day, the annual loss of revenue will be $8,176 (80 × 365 = 29,200 orders per year; 29,200 × .28 = $8,176). If the extra ounce is served in each order for other menu items, the cost to the restaurant could be impossible to absorb. Situation 2.6 presents an example of yield test and portion control. It emphasizes the impact that the cost of one extra ounce of servable product can have on the bottom line.

SITUATION 2.6 Yield Test and Portion Cost Control

As the manager of a restaurant specializing in roast beef sandwiches, you have been asked by your regional manager to analyze the profit margin of sandwiches sold.

The servable weight of bone-in top round of beef is 55 percent after cooking, carving, and bone loss. The purchase cost is $1.85 per pound. Each roast beef sandwich takes 8 ounces of servable meat. The sandwich sells for $6.99. The cost of the bun in which the meat is served, the jus, and the condiments is $0.45. Your maximum food cost allowed for this menu item is 28 percent.

ASSIGNMENT: Calculate the food cost percentage of the roast beef sandwich. Find out if reducing the amount of servable meat from 8 to 7 ounces would decrease the food cost percentage up to or below the preestablished 28 percent.

SERVICE IN FOOD OPERATIONS

Because of the intense competition faced by food operations in most locations, excellent service is a necessary component of the overall success formula. The quality of food offered by an establishment as well as its competitive prices, pleasant atmosphere, and easy access and parking will not be sufficient to please guests if service is poor. As frontline employees are in direct contact with guests, managers need to provide them with the necessary training, motivation, and **empowerment**—a management approach that gives employees the authority to provide effective service to customers. This is directly related to **total quality management (TQM)**, a theory emphasizing the achievement of guest satisfaction by empowering employees.

The essence of service is the anticipation of customers' needs. Fine dining service requires that qualified servers, chefs de rang, stay at their stations in the dining room at all times during the meal while their assistants, **commis de rang**, go back and forth to the kitchen. The idea is to foresee the diners' needs before they happen. Graduates joining the food service industry must develop a keen sense in order to provide courteous, genuinely friendly service. Situations 2.7 and 2.8 are examples of service situations commonly found in food operations.

SITUATION 2.7 The Missing Back Change

Sally Haviland has been working for Old Spaghetti Factory Restaurants for seven months. As a graduate from a 4-year hospitality program, Sally understands the importance service has in the hospitality industry. Today is Sunday and she has been entrusted with the supervision of the dinner service because her boss has called in sick with a bad cold. The restaurant is packed and the pace is frantic.

Sally was helping change one of the soda canisters in the beverage dispensing machine when she got a call from the cashier on duty. She hurries to the stand to find the cashier arguing with a middle-aged guest who is insisting that he was short-changed $20 by one of the servers. "I gave the waiter a $50 bill, my check was $12.50 and I only got back $17.50. Here it is, a ten, a five, two dollars and two quarters."

Several people are lining up waiting to be seated. Two customers are standing nearby, wanting to hand their bills to the cashier. Eager to know both sides of the story, Sally asks the cashier to step aside and quietly asks her what actually happened. The cashier offers this explanation: "He's lying. I'm absolutely sure that I gave the correct change to the waiter. The waiter insists that he gave the exact due-back amount to him—that is, $37.50.

ASSIGNMENT: Being in Sally's position, how would you proceed?

SITUATION 2.8   Customers' Special Requests

You have been trained as an assistant food and beverage manager at a Sheraton Hotel in Seattle, Washington. It is Sunday, and you are managing the breakfast service in the hotel's main dining room. The restaurant is very busy, with some 25 orders backed up in the kitchen. The **sous-chef** on duty and all **line cooks** are frantically filling out restaurant and room service orders.

William Collins, a regular **VIP** local customer, has brought to the hotel a party of five friends from France for the specific purpose of eating **eggs Benedict**, a specialty dish that he was served at the Sheraton at a private breakfast meeting 2 months ago. Wanting to please Mr. Collins, you take the order to the sous-chef for preparation. The sous-chef politely explains to you that the kitchen is understaffed and that making the hollandaise sauce for the dish will delay filling out the regular breakfast orders. According to him, the restaurant's service would be backed up 30 minutes if he has to leave the line to prepare the special request. He insists that it would be a bad idea to do so, given the situation.

ASSIGNMENT: What decision would you take as dining room manager?

KEY CONCEPTS/TERMS

à la carte	beurre manié
à la minute	butler service
banquet kitchen	casual dining
béarnaise sauce	château potatoes
béchamel sauce	chef de rang

cherries jubilée
choron sauce
commis de rang
cycle menu
dining room captain
Dubarry
dumbwaiter
eggs Benedict
empowerment
en papillote
entrée
espagnole sauce
ethnic restaurant
family restaurant
fillet
French cuisine
garniture
hollandaise sauce
kirschwasser

line cook
mise en place
napped
nouvelle cuisine
panaché de legumes
potage
quick service restaurant
rechaud
roux
sommelier
sous-chef
table d'hôte menu
tomato sauce
total quality management (TQM)
tournedos
velouté sauce
Véronique
very important person (VIP)

Chapter 3

Beverage Operations

CHAPTER OBJECTIVES

- Review the special aspects of beverage operations in lodging establishments, restaurants, bars, and coffeehouses.
- Discuss the characteristics of restaurant wine service.
- Calculate the potential revenue of a banquet bar.
- Determine the cost, price, and profit percentage of drinks.
- Resolve situational cases of beverage service operations.
- Discuss regulations for the sale of alcoholic drinks.

OVERVIEW

This chapter describes the special aspects of beverage operations in lodging establishments (hotels, resorts), restaurants (franchised, independent), bars (sports, pubs), and coffeehouses serving nonalcoholic beverages. Revenues from beverage sales provide hospitality operations with a substantial portion of the bottom line and a profit margin much higher than that for food. At the same time, the sale of alcoholic beverages presents some difficulties to managers because it is heavily regulated in most places and because of the responsibility and liability involved in the selling of intoxicating products to the public. The Dram Shop Acts, for instance, prohibit the sale of alcohol not only to minors but to adults who are visibly intoxicated. A breach of these regulations by service personnel may result in liability suits against the owner.

Managing beverage operations, and working in a place where people socialize, relax, and generally have a good time can however be an exciting experience. Companies that are recruiting at colleges and universities expect graduates to possess the basic knowledge to understand and supervise beverage operations. This knowledge should include being acquainted with wine and spirits service, product pricing and controls, and the regulations that apply to the sale of alcoholic beverages.

BEVERAGE SERVICE IN LODGING OPERATIONS

Besides generating substantial profits, the main purpose of serving beverages in lodging establishments is to provide a service to guests before, during, and after they patronize the property's food outlets. Often, servers at restaurants in large hotels and resorts place drink orders in the **service bar**—a bar that prepares drinks for table service only and is often not open to the public. It is usually a single, out-of-sight station that requires an expert bartender capable of filling different types of drink orders with great speed.

Wine Service

Students recruited to work in restaurants should have learned the different aspects of alcoholic beverage service. An important component of this service is wine. Although wine can be simply described as the fermented juice of grapes, there is a mystique about it that can be understood only by experience. At the very least, students should have some knowledge about the world's most important winegrowing regions and the winemaking process as well as the attributes of wine by type (various degrees of aromas, bouquets, and character) and the matching of wine with different types of foods. In the United States, a property's **house wines**—generic wine usually sold by the glass or in carafes—usually fall into three categories: (1) **Chablis** for white wines, (2) **Burgundy** for reds, and (3) **rosé** for pinks. Although these categories are generally accepted, they might be misleading because Chablis and Burgundy are wine-production regions of France and house wines served in America can be grown in any part of the world. Sometimes alcohol (usually **brandy**) is added to wines to produce **fortified wines**. Although the alcohol content by volume in table wines usually ranges from 10 to 14, fortified wines can be much stronger. These wines are served as **aperitifs** (**vermouth**, **pastis**) or **dessert wines** (**sherry**, **Marsala**). Students going into the industry should be reminded that wines are not only an excellent complement to a meal but also a way to substantially increase the profit percentage in restaurants.

SITUATION 3.1   Matching Wine with Food Dishes

Paul Evans has been recruited by the Hyatt Corporation to be assistant restaurant manager at a hotel in downtown Chicago. After 6 months of initial training, Paul is working as acting manager on weekends. While he is on duty on a Saturday afternoon, an important local business executive, Margaret Carlson, asks to see the restaurant manager to select a menu for a dinner she is hosting that evening for guests from out of town. After a lengthy discussion with Paul, she decides on the following menu:

Oysters Rockefeller
Salade Niçoise
Rack of Lamb Bouquetière
Pont Neuf Potatoes
Crème Caramel

Ms. Carlson asks Paul to select two of the best quality French wines from the wine list to be served with the meal: one with the oysters and one with the entrée. She also wants a "not-so-dry" champagne to be served with the dessert. Ms. Carlson also wants to know, before the meal, all about the wines so that she can answer questions from her guests. Paul rushes the order to the chef and begins to peruse the restaurant's wine list. The following French wines are offered:

Whites:
Côte de Beaune, Aloxe-Corton
Côte de Beaune, Meursalt
Alsace, Traminer
Chablis, Les Clos
Graves, Domaine de Chevalier
Sauternes, Barsac

Reds:
Saint-Emilion, Château Belair
Pomerol, Château La Pointe
Côte de Nuits, Chambertin
Côte de Beaune, Pommard
Beaujolais, Fleurie

Champagne:
Möet et Chandon, Brut
Veuve Clicquot-Ponsardin, Demi-sec

ASSIGNMENT: Select two wines from the above list that Paul Evans might choose—one for the oysters and one for the lamb—as well as a "not-so-dry" champagne to be served with the crème caramel. Be prepared to explain to Ms. Carlson the wine-producing regions that your selections originate from and the main characteristics of the wines chosen.

Banquet Service

Banquets and special functions, such as receptions and weddings, are an integral part of most lodging operations. Alcoholic beverages are usually served before, during, and after the function. Some hosts request the setup of a **cash bar**—drink service where guests pay cash to the bartender or are issued tickets to pay for the drinks. Others arrange for a **host bar**—drink service where guests are not charged but the organizer pays according to a preset price for the number of drinks served. Another option is to charge the host by the number of bottles opened and consumed. Beverage service in functions is provided from stations strategically set up around the room or from portable bars. An adequate mise en place is required to be able to serve a large number of guests in a short period of time. Bartenders must know the ingredients needed for a variety of drinks and the techniques for mixing them. Ideally, bartenders should be capable of working with both arms at the same time to cope with a high-volume service. Because the demand for banquets is not always steady, it is advisable for dining operations to have a list of **on-call workers**—both banquet servers and bartenders—to be available for such functions.

The control of revenue in banquet bars is usually challenging. Managers should ascertain that the total amount of money collected matches the quantity of alcoholic beverages served. One way to achieve control is to work out the potential revenue of the goods consumed and compare it with the actual revenue obtained. If bartenders know that the potential revenue is not calculated, they may feel free to overpour or, even worse, to pilfer from some of the cash taken in. In order to control revenue, each banquet bar setup is provided with a sheet listing the number of bottles of alcoholic beverages issued by category—liquor, wine, and beer. After the function is over, the returns are counted and the net use of each category ascertained; the potential revenue can then be figured out by multiplying the preestablished sales revenue per bottle by the number of bottles used. This revenue is usually calculated by assuming 1.5 ounces of liquor per drink and 6 ounces of wine per serving, although the serving size may vary by establishment. In all cases, the approximate number of ounces per liter is 33.8. Obviously, the price per drink varies from one operation to another.

SITUATION 3.2   Calculation of Potential Banquet Bar Revenue

Paul Evans has been promoted to banquet manager at the Hyatt Corporation's downtown Chicago hotel. Today, he is in the process of setting up a portable cash bar for a Shriners' function. The bar service will include the items shown below:

Item	Size	Number of Items
House bourbon	1.5 L	5 bottles
House scotch	1.5 L	5 bottles
Call vodka	1.0 L	3 bottles
Call rum	1.0 L	2 bottles
Call gin	1.0 L	2 bottles
Call scotch	1.0 L	3 bottles
Call bourbon	1.0 L	4 bottles
House red wine	1.5 L	6 bottles
House white wine	1.5 L	5 bottles
House rosé wine	1.5 L	3 bottles
Domestic beer	12 oz	10 × 24 case
Imported beer	12 oz	10 × 12 pack

At the end of the function, the following items were returned:

Item	Full	Empty	Partial	Potential Sales per Bottle
House bourbon	2	2	0.6	$123.75
House scotch	3	1	0.2	123.75
Call vodka	0	3	None	82.50
Call rum	1	0	0.5	82.50
Call gin	0	1	0.1	82.50
Call scotch	2	0	0.2	82.50
Call bourbon	0	4	None	82.50
House red wine	2	4	None	28.90
House white wine	4	0	0.3	28.90
House rosé wine	3	0	None	28.90
Domestic beer	90 units			2.75
Imported beer	85 units			3.75

ASSIGNMENT: Calculate the potential income of the cash bar, and find out the percentage difference with the actual revenue. The sales for the evening totaled $2,031.50.

BEVERAGE SERVICE IN RESTAURANTS

As stated before, the beverage service in restaurants is a critical part of the overall income of the establishment—the profit margin from beverages being much higher than that from food. Restaurant patrons often like to enjoy a drink or two while sitting at a bar before or after dining. In some restaurants, the bar is a focal point where guests meet other guests, watch sports on nearby television screens, or simply have a drink while winding down from a day's work.

In the dining room, customers enjoy having a drink or a glass of wine with their dinner. The wines featured must complement the restaurant's menu, and they must be compatible in price with the cost of the dishes and fit the type of clientele. Some restaurants offering an uncomplicated menu may serve only house wines by the glass or by the **carafe**—a glass container used to serve wine. Fine-dining establishments must have an extensive selection of domestic and imported wines. In all cases, wines must be properly merchandised and the servers efficiently trained to optimize sales. Besides the wine list, restaurants often place table tents and display blackboards at the restaurant's entrance to attract the attention of customers. The pricing of wines is relatively simple. Restaurants usually follow the rule of thumb of tripling the cost of inexpensive wines and just doubling the cost of expensive wines in order to make the price affordable to guests. In both cases, the effect on the bottom line is equivalent; for instance, a bottle whose cost to the property is $5.00 that sells for $15.00 (the cost having been tripled) will generate the same profit as a bottle that costs $10 and is sold for $20 (the cost having been doubled).

Recent graduates from hospitality schools working in the beverage segment of the industry must understand that their main challenge is to offer the larger part of their clientele the atmosphere and the type of drinks they prefer at prices that are acceptable. It is not advisable, for example, to feature Dewar's White Label Scotch as a pouring brand in an establishment patronized by a lower-middle-class clientele. Another important goal for managers is to maximize profits. In order to achieve an optimum bottom line, they have to be proficient in pricing the products sold. The essence of pricing is to sell drinks at a sum that is acceptable to guests and that maximizes the difference between a drink's cost and its sales price.

Each drink sold at a bar should be priced to achieve a preestablished **gross profit**—the amount resulting from subtracting the cost of sales from total sales. Generally, the preestablished liquor cost percentage ranges between 20 and 25 percent of the sales price. The pricing involves **costing the recipe**—calculating the cost of a drink's ingredients divided by the preestablished cost percentage. The process is relatively simple when calculating prices for straight drinks but can be complex when working out the cost of mixed drinks.

SITUATION 3.3   Pricing a Mixed Drink

Verna McNeill has been hired as assistant bar manager of the main bar of a luxury hotel in New York City. Her first assignment is to price the mixed drinks featured on the bar's cocktail menu to obtain a 25 percent cost percentage. Verna knows that she first has to cost the recipe and then divide the amount by the cost percentage. She begins with **daiquiri**, a sweet-sour mixed drink that at that particular bar is prepared using the following recipe:

   1 jigger (1.5 oz) Bacardi rum
   1 jigger lime juice
   1 tsp sugar (1/6 oz)

The rum is poured from a 1-liter bottle that costs $9.75. One lime is used, on average, to fill a jigger of juice. The cost of one lime is 15 cents. The cost of 1 pound of sugar is $1.90.

ASSIGNMENT: Determine the sales price of the daiquiri to obtain the targeted 25 percent cost.

BEVERAGE SERVICE IN BARS

The concept to be adopted when opening a bar should follow **market research**— a study conducted to determine the needs of an area's customers. The results of the initial research should determine the décor, atmosphere, and beverage menu that the property should offer. Some guests like a relaxed environment where they can carry on a quiet conversation while others may prefer the hustle and bustle of a nightclub offering salsa music. Unlike bars in restaurants, some enterprises are designed to serve beverages only, with no food or a very limited menu offered. These are usually neighborhood gathering places where people play darts or pool or just sit placidly by a fireplace. It is common for this type of bar to feature signature drinks that are different or better prepared than in other establishments. Other liquor-only establishments are characterized by the ambience inspired by the décor, the amiability of bartenders and servers, the music, or the idiosyncratic clientele. Some people may feel comfortable in a western-style saloon while others may prefer the atmosphere of a Mexican cantina.

New managers working in beverage operations must be aware of the possibility that bartenders may steal sales revenue. This is made easy by the fact that bartenders prepare the product while collecting and recording revenues as well. For instance, they can underpour or dilute liquor to get more drinks out of a bottle without affecting the beverage cost percentage. Another way for bartenders to pilfer is by improperly using the cash register. Typical examples are collecting money from guests and registering it as "no-ring sales" or, if paid with the exact amount, pocketing the money and not using the cash register at all. Closing down the register after the end of every shift should include the procedure of using a cashier's checkout slip to reconcile the total register sales with the cash and credit vouchers.

SITUATION 3.4   Reconciling Register Sales with Actual Cash, Credit Slips, and Vouchers

As the manager on duty at a restaurant in San Antonio, you have been asked to audit the beverage sales for the evening shift at the bar. The beginning bank for the shift was $150. The cash register contains the following cash, credit slips, and vouchers:

Bills	$ 500.25
Coins	55.05
Credit card slips	191.60
Payout voucher	22.50 (ice cube bags)
Comped by management	9.25
Signed by general manager	12.40
Customer skip	28.00
Overring	409.00
Total sales on register tape	1,079.05

ASSIGNMENT: Calculate the actual over or short.

BEVERAGE SERVICE IN COFFEEHOUSES

A trend in the beverage industry is the recent proliferation of places where people gather to consume nonalcoholic drinks, particularly coffee and tea. Some of these establishments feature several types of coffee grown around the world, traditional teas from Ceylon and China, a profusion of herbal infusions, and a variety of healthy juices. Properties offering computers with Internet access for professional and leisure use are also popular with tourists, teenagers and college students. Some of these enterprises are independently owned and others are chains or franchises such as Starbucks. Because of the size and limited investment needed to open and operate coffeehouses, some students nearing graduation express interest in opening their own establishments. In most cases they need to raise the funds from investors (often relatives or friends of the family) who put the money into the business in exchange for a share of its ownership. Most likely, the investors will ask for their expected **return on investment (ROI)**—a ratio obtained by calculating the profit goal of the operation and the amount invested.

SITUATION 3.5   Evaluating Return on Investment

Ruth Anderson, a senior at a hotel and restaurant management program in Nevada, wants to own and operate a sports bar in Las Vegas. Ruth has found an establishment for sale that is well located near the university. Using her father's assets as collateral, she can obtain a bank loan for the purchase of the property, a light remodeling, and the initial working capital. The equity investment was calculated at $1,100,000. Ruth estimated that the average return on the investment should be about 18 percent annually after income taxes for the project to be feasible.

Ruth has worked out a pro forma income statement for the first 3 years of operations that looks like this:

	Year 1	Year 2	Year 3
Operating income	$1,277,500	$1,405,250	$1,545,775
Fixed charges	1,337,000	1,117,000	842,000
Income before taxes	(59,500)	288,250	703,775
Income tax	—	115,300	316,700
Net income (loss)	(59,500)	172,950	387,075

ASSIGNMENT: Given the estimates of revenue and expenses, work out the average yearly return on the initial $1,100,000 equity investment and advise Ruth on whether or not to go ahead with the operation.

SERVICE IN BEVERAGE OPERATIONS

Although the hospitality industry is committed to providing excellent service and accommodating its customers' needs, this premise is at times difficult to maintain when customers consume too much alcohol. In order for customers to patronize an establishment, they must feel that they will be reasonably safe from guests who exhibit unruly behavior. Intoxicated guests may make abusive advances toward the establishment's workers or commit acts against the property's assets—for example, harassing servers or vandalizing or stealing equipment or supplies. In these cases management must act decisively to restore order, cutting these patrons off from ordering drinks or expelling them from the premises. Recent graduates from hospitality schools may find it difficult to deal with belligerent guests who are often much older than they are.

SITUATION 3.6   Dealing with Patrons Showing Abusive Behavior Toward Servers

Jack Murphy is considered a good, steady customer in the bar where you are working as supervisor. In the past, he has brought considerable business from his company. Today, you notice that he is ordering double whiskies instead of his regular draft beer. He seems to have developed a fondness for Karen, one of your cocktail waitresses. Earlier in the evening, he allegedly started grabbing her and making unsolicited advances. He said that he was only joking. Now, Karen comes to you quite upset and says, "He's doing it again. I can't stand it any longer."

ASSIGNMENT: As the supervisor that evening, what would you do regarding the problem?

SITUATION 3.7   Dealing with Patrons Who Steal Equipment

It is happy hour. The bar where you are acting as manager on duty is packed. A cocktail waitress approaches you and says, "There are two glasses missing from table 7. I didn't see anyone taking them but look at the huge purse at the feet of that woman."

ASSIGNMENT: What would you do in this case? What would you do if the waitress had seen the patron put the two glasses in her purse?

REGULATIONS FOR THE SALE OF ALCOHOLIC DRINKS

There are several federal, state, and local laws that apply to the sale of alcoholic beverages. Graduates recruited to work in beverage operations must be aware of the rules and regulations that apply to the location where the establishment operates. Most states have regulations about the hours alcoholic beverages may be sold—for example, having to be closed during early-morning hours or closing for part of the day on Sunday. All states prohibit the sale of spirits to minors. Serving a minor is a major offense subject to fines and even the loss of license.

It is the responsibility of the operator to deny service to patrons who are clearly intoxicated; however, it is against the law to refuse to serve a customer on the basis of race, creed, color, sex, or national origin. In order to avoid charges of discrimination, it is advisable to have a witness who verifies that the person is indeed intoxicated. Most states enforce **third-party liability**— potential liability under the Dram Shop Acts laws making the person who sells liquor to a minor or intoxicated person, not the drinker, liable for injuries caused by that person's drunkenness.

In some states, the sale of distilled products is a monopoly of the state, meaning that operators must buy only from stores owned by the state. In other states, operators must buy products from licensed suppliers. In some states, certain container sizes cannot be sold. Periodic on-premise inspections by federal agents guarantee that the content of the liquor bottle corresponds to what the label states. When opening a bottle, part of its **strip stamp** must be left attached to the bottle's neck and the content of the bottle must not be transferred to any other bottle. Adding other spirits or another substance to an open bottle is forbidden. Reusing an empty spirits bottle for any purpose is against federal law.

SITUATION 3.8   How Much Liquor Consumption Is Enough?

It is 9 o'clock in the evening. As manager on duty at a hotel near the Denver airport, you have been asked by Tony, the bartender, to report to the Applause lounge. A loud discussion is taking place between a guest and Tony. Several of the patrons standing at the counter and seated at the tables are paying attention to what is going on. The atmosphere seems to be tense.

The guest—a tall, sturdy gentleman crowned by a large Stetson hat and dressed in blue jeans and a checkered shirt—is recriminating Tony for refusing to serve him another drink. He doesn't appear to be drunk and his speech is quite intelligible. He is arguing that he is used to drinking and that his weight allows him to drink more than a "regular" person. Tony claims that the customer has been drinking since happy hour began and that in his opinion he has had more alcohol that he can handle.

Trying to be conciliatory, you offer the gentleman a cup of coffee on the house. He immediately refuses and requests another drink before driving home for the night. You then ask Tony to serve him the drink, telling the customer that this will definitely be the last one.

ASSIGNMENT: Discuss and critique this case.

KEY CONCEPTS/TERMS

aperitif	house wine
brandy	market research
Burgundy	Marsala
carafe	on-call workers
cash bar	pastis
Chablis	return on investment
costing the recipe	rosé
daiquiri	service bar
dessert wine	sherry
fortified wine	strip stamp
gross profit	third-party liability
host bar	vermouth

Chapter 4

Housekeeping Operations

CHAPTER OBJECTIVES

- Review the importance of adequate staffing of employees.
- Determine productivity standards for housekeeping workers.
- Practice measuring section housekeeper productivity.
- Determine linen par and inventory exercises.
- Describe aspects of laundry room supervision.
- Resolve an operational situation on expense control.

OVERVIEW

This chapter deals with some of the diverse situations that graduates from hotel and restaurant management programs face when hired by lodging companies to work in housekeeping departments. Complex to manage and less than glamorous, the housekeeping department, along with the front office, is an intrinsic part of the rooms division, determining the success or failure of the property's operation. While the income of the F&B division is usually 20 to 25 percent of its sales, that of the rooms division generally reaches 70 to 80 percent of the revenue obtained from selling guest rooms. These high percentages can be achieved by realizing the highest possible average daily rate (ADR) (a task that pertains to the front office and sales departments) and by minimizing operating expenses (a task that depends mostly on the cost control efforts of a qualified housekeeping department management team). The lodging industry prefers to hire housekeeping managers who can perform as first-line managers, capable of directing housekeeping departments by themselves without the direct intervention of the property's upper management. These positions require that individuals have a thorough knowledge of the technical aspects of housekeeping operations and that they be proficient in managing resources (including human) and in administering assets.

Recruiting lodging companies often hire graduates from hotel and restaurant management programs to place them in starting positions in housekeeping departments. Students looking for hospitality jobs should consider accepting these job offers as they provide an excellent opportunity for new employees to prove themselves competent in the operation of a department that generally employs the largest number of people in a lodging establishment. Specifically, recruiters of lodging companies look for graduates with knowledge in staffing workers effectively, administering resources, supervising the laundry department, and controlling expenses. Overall, the operational goals of housekeeping managers and supervisors are to maximize quality standards while minimizing costs.

MANAGING LABOR IN THE HOUSEKEEPING DEPARTMENT

The task of having to service a large number of checkout rooms in a short period of time to accommodate the guests checking in can be challenging. It is not uncommon in lodging properties to have most of the guest rooms vacate around midday and the majority of the day's arrivals check in at about the same time. Considering that each room must be thoroughly cleaned and inspected as quickly as possible, it is clear that the scheduling of **rooms division** employees is not an easy matter.

Because labor is the largest of housekeeping expenses, housekeeping management must be careful not to overschedule the department's workforce because calling too many employees to work results in decreased departmental profit. At the same time, not having enough workers to turn over rooms that are ready to the front desk will result in complaints from incoming guests, causing an eventual loss of business. Thus, when scheduling workers, a balance between the need to provide adequate coverage to clean effectively and to obtain the budgeted labor cost percentages must be achieved.

SITUATION 4.1   Forecasting Monthly Housekeeping Labor Costs

Paul Sandoval has been working as assistant to the executive housekeeper at a 624-room resort in Fort Lauderdale, Florida, for six months. Paul has been left in charge of the department for the 2 weeks while his boss is on vacation. On May 3, he receives a call from Carol Compton, the property's controller, requesting a labor cost forecast for the month of June. Paul is told that the budgeted revenue for the month has been downgraded because of the cancellation of three large conventions that had been previously booked. The resort, however, expects to increase the number of transient guests and obtain a higher **average daily rate (ADR)** than previously budgeted for. Carol provides Paul with the following information:

Budgeted occupancy for June	90%
Budgeted ADR for June	$95
New occupancy forecast for June	75%
New ADR for June	$105
Average **section housekeeper** hourly wage	$7.15

Budgeted monthly **team supervisors** and **housepersons** labor cost	$24,100
Budgeted monthly laundry labor cost	$19,760
Budgeted monthly **fixed team** labor cost	$11,800
Budgeted monthly **evening team** labor cost	$7,100
Budgeted monthly **management team** salaries	$10,400

Paul knows that the **section housekeeper workload** for one 8-hour shift is 15 rooms and that the budgeted labor cost percentage (not including payroll taxes and benefits) was 8.5 percent of total sales. He decides not to change the labor cost for the fixed team or for the management team but to reduce the laundry labor cost by 15 percent and the supervisor/houseperson's by 8 percent to compensate for the decrease in number of rooms sold.

ASSIGNMENT: Calculate the new projected revenue for the month of June, the new total departmental labor cost in dollars, and the new labor cost percentage to total room sales.

Productivity

The productivity of housekeeping employees is measured by **productivity standards**—the average output of workers during a fixed period of time according to a preestablished quality criterion. For example, if it is determined that to clean an average guest room takes section housekeepers 32 minutes on average, workers are made accountable for servicing a specific number of guest rooms during their shift.

SITUATION 4.2   Determining Productivity Standards

Paul Sandoval's new project is to establish more accurate productivity standards for section housekeepers at the resort. He first determines how long it should take a section housekeeper to clean one guest room according to the department's performance standards. He decides that on average, one guestroom can be cleaned in 32 minutes. He takes into consideration that section housekeepers need 15 minutes at the beginning of the shift, and 15 minutes at the end of the shift for preparation before and after the actual cleaning begins. Each worker is allowed one midmorning break of 15 minutes and 30 minutes for lunch. The shifts consist of 8 hours on the clock.

ASSIGNMENT: Determine the productivity standard as measured by the number of guest rooms that should be cleaned by each section housekeeper in one 8-hour shift.

One way to measure the productivity of the section housekeepers in lodging operations is to compare the average time spent in cleaning guest rooms with the average time allocated in the budget for this task. That is, if the budget's target is 28 minutes per room on average and section housekeepers are taking an average of 37 minutes, productivity has decreased; if the average time is below 28 minutes, productivity has increased.

SITUATION 4.3   Measuring Section Housekeeper Productivity

Paul Sandoval wants to compare the productivity of his section housekeepers with the projected budget. He will measure the average time it took to clean guest rooms at the resort during the week of May 16–22. The number of rooms occupied during the week was 3,708; the number of section housekeeper hours for the week (taken from the department time cards) was 1,976 hours. The budgeted average time to clean a room at the resort had been set at 35 minutes.

ASSIGNMENT: Was the productivity of the section housekeepers below or above budget? By how many minutes per room cleaned on average?

MANAGEMENT OF HOUSEKEEPING ASSETS

The amount of material used in the housekeeping department is considerable. Executive housekeepers are responsible for the administration, maintenance, and control of guest room furniture, equipment and supplies.

Pars

A **par** is the ideal number of items to have in stock in order to ensure that enough are available for daily operations. The executive housekeeper must establish pars for linen, **cleaning supplies**—the products and utensils used for cleaning—and **guest supplies**—complimentary items provided for guests. In the case of **bed linens**, for example, a par of three is recommended. This means that ideally three sets of pillowcases and sheets must be kept on hand at all times; usually, one set in each guest room, a second set being laundered, and a third set ready to go in room closets and section housekeeper carts. An additional number of sheets and pillow cases might be kept on reserve under lock and key.

SITUATION 4.4   Setting Up Linen Pars

Grace Washington has been recruited by the Hyatt Corporation to work in the housekeeping department of a hotel in San Francisco. Grace has been assigned the job of working out the number of bed linens and **terry cloth items** that need to be kept on hand for a par stock of 3.5. The hotel has 685 guest rooms—400 with two queen beds in each room and 285 with one king bed. The establishment uses two sheets per bed, two standard-size pillows for each queen bed, and three large-size pillows per king bed. The bathroom in each guest room is equipped with one bath mat. Four hand towels and four bath towels are placed in each queen/queen room and three hand towels and two bath towels in the king rooms.

ASSIGNMENT: How many pillowcases (by size), sheets (by size), hand towels, bath towels, and bath mats should Grace recommend to have on hand at the property for a par stock of 3.5?

Linen Inventories

Physical linen inventories must be conducted regularly in lodging properties (usually every month). The purpose of taking inventories is to determine the number of items needed to be purchased to bring stocks up to par; a second goal is to ascertain linen losses that may be taking place due to pilfering by employees and guests.

SITUATION 4.5   Linen Inventories

Grace Washington has now been asked to take the bed linen inventory for the month of June at the same hotel. After physically counting all sheets and pillowcases on hand, she compiles the list below.

	Queen Sheets	King Sheets	Standard Pillowcases	Large Pillowcases
Beginning inventory (6/1)	5,300	1,900	4,580	2,750
Purchased in June	144	—	180	240
In guest rooms (6/30)	1,600	570	1,600	855
In laundry room (6/30)	1,520	525	1,490	910
In floor closets (6/30)	800	418	840	740
In carts (6/30)	1,400	310	490	325
Discarded in June	9	—	50	13

ASSIGNMENT: Calculate the number of pieces that cannot be accounted for (shrinkage) and the number of items (by category) that need to be bought in order to bring the par to the numbers below.

Queen sheets	5,600
King sheets	1,995
Standard pillowcases	5,600
Large pillowcases	2,992

SUPERVISION OF LAUNDRY OPERATIONS

Although the supervision of laundry operations is usually delegated to a manager, executive housekeepers have the overall responsibility of this department. Graduates assigned to the housekeeping department must understand basic operations, from the collection of linens to the finished product, the characteristics of laundry equipment, the properties of laundry chemicals, and how to control operating costs.

Generally, the highest expense in laundry operations is labor, followed by linen replacement, energy, and laundry chemicals. An approximate distribution of laundry cost percentages in the industry can be summarized as follows:

Labor	45%
Linen replacement	20
Energy	20
Laundry chemicals	15

These benchmarks may vary substantially, depending on special circumstances—for example, if the cost of energy is particularly high where the property is located, if the equipment is obsolete or poorly maintained, or if the linen is of poor quality.

SITUATION 4.6   Laundry Operating Cost Control

Sam Hospodka, a recent graduate of a hotel and restaurant management program, has been hired by a lodging company as housekeeping supervisor. At a staff meeting Helen Cramer, the property's controller, raises the issue of costs for laundry operations, which apparently went up substantially last year. She distributes a graph to the department heads attending the meeting. The graph shows the following average cost percentages for the last 5 years:

Labor	44%
Linen replacement	21
Energy	20
Laundry chemicals	15

Last year, the dollar cost was $134,500. The general manager suggests that Sam investigate the issue to find out the possible causes for the increase in laundry room expenses.

Sam requests a statement of last year's expenses and receives the following information:

Labor cost	$65,635
Linen replacement	25,900
Energy	23,800
Laundry chemicals	19,165

ASSIGNMENT: What was the probable cause of the cost increase in the laundry department last year? What suggestions should Sam propose to minimize expenses?

CONTROLLING EXPENSES IN THE HOUSEKEEPING DEPARTMENT

The major expense categories that housekeeping managers must control, besides salaries and wages, are cleaning and laundry supplies, guest supplies, and linen replacement. The **cost per occupied room** is a good determinant of expenses per room sold. The cost is obtained by dividing each expense category for a certain period of time by the number of rooms sold during that period of time. The figure obtained will be compared with that projected in the budget and will provide information about whether or not too much money is being spent.

SITUATION 4.7   Controlling Expenditures on Guest Supplies

Three years after having been hired by a 2,526-room hotel in Las Vegas, Jocelyn Peralta is promoted to executive housekeeper. Eager to provide guests with a memorable stay at the hotel, Jocelyn has recommended an upgrade of the **nonreusable guest supplies**—items used by guests only once—including adding a box of Perugina chocolates in each guest room per stay. Jocelyn was asked by management to provide the annual additional cost of guest supplies to the hotel that the upgrade would represent, indicating that in no case should the extra expense be more than 5 percent of the current cost per occupied room. The average cost per room for the past 5 years has been $3.15. After preparing the budget forecast for the next fiscal year, Jocelyn requested $250,392 to cover the additional cost of the new nonreusable amenities. The hotel's occupancy forecast for the year was as follows:

January	72%
February	79
March	81
April	94

May	94
June	95
July	99
August	97
September	85
October	62 (room refurbishing projected)
November	65
December	83

ASSIGNMENT: Calculate the projected new cost per room for nonreusable guest supplies and ascertain whether Jocelyn's increase of $250,392 for the year will be approved by management.

KEY CONCEPTS/TERMS

average daily rate (ADR)	management team
bed linens	nonreusable guest supplies
cleaning supplies	par
cost per occupied room	productivity standard
evening team	rooms division
fixed team	section housekeeper
guest amenities	section housekeeper workload
guest supplies	team supervisor
houseperson	terry cloth items

Chapter 5

Front Office Operations

CHAPTER OBJECTIVES

- Review the overall functions of the front office.
- Discuss the conundrum of overbooking.
- Understand the need to maximize occupancy and average daily rate (ADR).
- Practice the concept of yield management.
- Discuss the rationale for room pricing.
- Practice room count and night audit procedures.

OVERVIEW

This chapter focuses on situations commonly encountered by graduates joining the front office operations in lodging establishments. Because the front office is at the hub of activities where most guest transactions take place, students are eager to be recruited for positions in this department where a constant stream of guests from all walks of life can be met in person. On a personal note, I have, for example, checked in and interacted with many celebrities, such as movie stars Brigitte Bardot, Raquel Welch, Claudia Cardinale, Jack Hawkins, George C. Scott, Stephen Boyd, Eli Wallach, Sean Connery, and Jim Brown as well as cellist Gaspar Cassado and film directors Sergio Leone, Edward Dmytrick, and John Guillermine.

Students interviewing for positions at the front office must have the skills to communicate with all kinds of travelers and be able and willing to deal with the complex situations that front-line employees must deal with. As part of the property's rooms division, the front office includes, in most large operations, the front desk, reservations, and uniformed services (bell staff) departments. The main functions of the front office are to provide services directly to guests, to maintain a detailed up-to-the-minute inventory of guest rooms, and to keep accurate records of business transactions.

SUPERVISION OF THE FRONT DESK DEPARTMENT

Besides providing services to guests, the main goal of the front desk, in close cooperation with the reservations and sales departments, is to sell as many guest rooms as possible at the highest feasible rate. The manager or shift supervisor must strive each day to achieve 100 percent occupancy by combining reservations booked in advance with the up-to-the-moment call-in and walk-in sales. In order to sell out the property, front desk supervisors must take calculated risks, involving the possibility of **walking a guest**—rejecting a guest who has a confirmed reservations. Although some lodging companies have standing policies against **overbooking**—taking a larger number of reservations than rooms are available for the same period—the most common practice in the industry is to attempt to fill every room in the house every day. Situation 5.1 deals with the dilemma of accepting over-the-limit reservations risking the possibility of walking guests.

SITUATION 5.1   Overbooking

Andrew Foster is supervising the evening shift at a 235-room hotel located near the Anaheim Convention Center. At 10:58 PM, he receives a call from the visitor's center at the Long Beach Municipal Airport requesting two rooms for the night for a VIP and his family who have just missed their outbound flight. Andrew asks the caller to stay on the line while he finds out whether he can risk accepting the reservation. Looking at the status report on the computer screen, he reads the following:

Rooms occupied	230
Rooms out of order	1
Guaranteed arrivals	6
Rooms available	−2

Andrew knows that according to the historical record for the hotel, 5 percent of the daily reservations are **no-shows**—persons who have failed to register as scheduled. The total reservations for the day has been 146 rooms.

Andrew has always been nervous about having to make overbooking decisions. These situations remind him of the ethics discussions he had in college on whether or not to take advantage of guests in order to improve the bottom line. At the same time, he is also aware of the standing policy for the front desk to sell out every night if at all possible.

Andrew digs into the **reservations bucket**—the container where reservations are filed. He pulls out the paperwork for the six reservations remaining for the night. They show the following:

2 rooms—Mastercard-guaranteed for late arrival.

1 room—Letter signed by the front office manager 3 months ago confirming the reservation for a business executive from Peru. No credit card guarantee.

2 rooms—Visa-guaranteed reservation made by a local travel agency.

1 room—Reservation made by the hotel's sales manager for a **meeting planner**—a person employed by corporations, organizations, or entities to book conventions and other functions.

Andrew knows that he is already two rooms in the hole. Nevertheless, recognizing that it is almost midnight he decides to make sure that the hotel is sold out that night. He goes back to the phone and accepts the two rooms for the VIP at the airport. The hotel is now four rooms in the hole with six additional rooms reserved.

ASSIGNMENT: Consider the situation and argue in favor or against Andrew's decision. What would you do if one of the outstanding reservations shows up later that evening?

Together with optimizing guest room occupancy, the front desk must attempt to maximize rates. It is always easy for a lodging establishment to sell out at largely discounted prices but difficult to achieve the highest ADR possible while reaching substantial levels of occupancy. Situation 5.2 deals with the interrelationship between ADR and occupancy.

SITUATION 5.2   Relationship Between ADR and Occupancy Percentage

Su Hee Liu is the front office manager of a 229-room hotel in Seattle. At yesterday's staff meeting, the property's general manager spoke of the need to increase occupancy to boost revenues in the food and beverage outlets, particularly in the restaurant and bar areas. The GM would like to increase the projected 65 percent occupancy for the next 3 months to 75 percent by offering discounts. However, he insists on achieving the same budgeted revenue from room sales. The budgeted ADR for the period had been set at $115.

ASSIGNMENT: What decrease in dollars on the budgeted ADR can the hotel afford in order to increase the occupancy from 65 to 75 percent without lowering the budgeted revenue from guest room sales?

YIELD MANAGEMENT

Yield management (YM) is a revenue maximization technique that aims to increase net yields by allocating available room capacity at optimum price. In practice, YM has to do with the alignment of room price and guest demand; that is, rates are kept high when the demand is there and lowered (to attract buyers) when the demand is weak. However, high occupancy ratios at discounted rates are unsatisfactory if the property's profitability (yield) decreases.

SITUATION 5.3   Understanding Yield Management

At the end of the 90 days in which discounts to attract occupancy had been offered, the GM asked Su Hee Liu if the profitability had increased or decreased. Su Hee decides to put into practice his knowledge of yield management to find out the profitability percentage using the yield efficiency formula learned in college. The results for the 3-month period had been as follows:

Occupancy	78%
ADR	$89.40

ASSIGNMENT: Apply the yield efficiency formula and find out the difference between the expected yield and the yield actually achieved.

Rate Calculation

Graduates from hotel and restaurant programs will most likely find established rates at the lodging establishments where they are about to work. There are several variables involved in the determination of rates; for instance, location of the property, season, direct competition, and so on. Generally, the pricing is based on **market-based rate**—the average rate of guest rooms set after analysis of the variables listed above. Occasionally, recent graduates will be involved in the determination of room rates if they form part of a lodging operation's **opening team**—the employees selected by a company to open a new establishment. In this case, the starting rate should be a **cost-based rate** and take into consideration the expected **return on investment (ROI)**—a ratio obtained by dividing profit by the owner's investment. The purpose of this calculation is to make sure that the minimum rate adopted allows for the project to be financially sound.

SITUATION 5.4   Cost-Based Rate Calculation

After several years as an industry professional, Mark Spencer has been assigned the job of coordinator of the opening team of a 310-room hotel soon to be inaugurated in Portland, Oregon. The corporate office has asked Mark to determine the minimal initial average room rate needed to cover the total expenses and the company's projected ROI (15 percent of the initial $15,450,000 capital investment). Mr. Spencer was provided with the figures listed below:

ROI	$2,317,500
Tax	927,000
Annual property and operating costs	3,181,000
Interest	1,100,000

Income (profit) from other departments	1,236,000
Estimated rooms division expenses	2,695,500

Information received from the sales department indicates that the annual occupancy for the first year has been estimated at 62 percent.

ASSIGNMENT: What is the minimum ADR that the property needs to adopt given the ROI and the operations predictions listed above?

SUPERVISION OF THE RESERVATIONS DEPARTMENT

Although small lodging operations usually process room reservations at the front desk, medium- and large-sized establishments generally have a reservations department in charge of this task. In all cases, the reservations department is part of the property's front office structure. The main purpose of the reservations department is to match room requests with room availability, to confirm and maintain reservations records, and to prepare room-availability forecasts and reports.

The reservations staff must work in strict synchronization with the front desk and the sales department and with out-of-the-property central reservation systems (if any) as the sale of rooms may be going on in various locations 24 hours a day. Keeping an accurate up-to-the-minute inventory of rooms available is therefore a challenging task. The reservation process, however, is simplified if the property's computerized system is interfaced with all originators of reservations.

Lodging companies often place new rooms division recruits in reservations departments. It is important that future front office managers have a clear understanding of the process of accommodating guests from the moment they make a call for a reservation until the time they check into the property. Today, most lodging properties use high-tech systems to post and maintain reservation records. At a touch of a key, status reports and forecasts can be conveniently generated. Manager-trainees, however, should have a thorough understanding of how computers process the inputted information.

Forecasts and Daily Room Counts

Forecasts and daily room counts are important in lodging properties for several reasons. In addition to calculating the number of rooms available to be sold at any given moment, such counts provide information to other departments necessary for the scheduling of employees and the procurement of foodstuffs and supplies. For example, the F&B director needs to know the approximate daily number of guests staying in the hotel in order to staff all outlets efficiently; the executive chef purchases food items ahead of time based on the hotel's occupancy; the executive housekeeper requires information on rooms sold to anticipate guest room cleaning schedules. Short-range forecasts are issued by the front office weekly, with copies sent to the GM, all department heads, and the members of the **executive committee**.

Daily Room Count

Because of the fluctuations of incoming reservations, date changes, and cancellations that take place constantly in lodging operations, the weekly forecast is adjusted on a daily basis to obtain a fairly accurate count of rooms available. Usually this procedure takes place first thing in the morning and includes historical trends for no-shows, **overstays**, **understays**, and **cancellations**. The historical trends are figured out from averaged-out data gathered over long periods of time. These trends are in turn influenced by factors such as special local events, season, location of the property, and weather. Reservations managers develop a feel for predicting (in most cases accurately) the ups and downs of room availability. Occasionally the prediction is off, resulting in overbooking or underselling guest rooms.

SITUATION 5.5   Daily Room Count

Vanessa McMahon has been working as reservations supervisor at a 346-room hotel in Nashville, Tennessee. It is Monday, May 5, and Vanessa has been asked by the reservations manager to prepare the hotel's room occupancy count for the day. The hotel's computers are down, and she has to gather and organize the filed written backup records for the day's arrivals. After tallying the reservations by category, she completes the following account:

Rooms occupied yesterday	302
Confirmed 4 PM reservations	15
Guaranteed for late-arrival reservations	273
Predicted checkouts for today	230
Rooms out of order	none

Historical records indicate that for weekdays in May the average no-shows for 4 PM reservations have been 12 percent and for late-arrival guaranteed reservations 2.2 percent. The average overstays for predicted checkouts have been 2 percent and the understays 6 percent. The predicted cancellations are 1 percent of the total reservations for the day.

ASSIGNMENT: What is the room count for May 5 at the beginning of the morning shift?

THE NIGHT AUDIT

Although most, if not all, lodging properties today use computerized control systems, technology is only as accurate as the data provided. It is therefore important that night auditors understand the process of account record keeping. A sudden failure of the property's computerized system should not be an obstacle for **balancing up**—the final calculation of the day's transactions done by the night auditor.

The night auditor shift provides an excellent opportunity for graduates to understand the accounting procedures that take place daily in lodging operations. No employee should try to be promoted to front desk manager without a complete grasp of how business transactions and vouchers are processed, how all records are reconciled and balanced to the penny before guests begin to check out the following morning, and how the various reports are generated.

Basically, the night audit is a detailed account of daily charges and credits added and subtracted to an **opening balance**—the accounts receivable amount brought forward from yesterday's business cycle—to obtain at the end of the day's business cycle **a closing balance**—the balance of all accounts for the day's business cycle. The two outstanding totals to be balanced by the night auditor are the **guest ledger** (unpaid bills or **guest folios** of staying guests) and the **city ledger** (unpaid accounts receivable by nonregistered guests, credit card companies, and **direct bill** accounts). When balancing the guest ledger, the total outstanding debit sum of registered guests obtained must equal the sum of all guest folios. When balancing the city ledger, the total outstanding debit sum of nonregistered guests obtained must equal the sum of all pending nonregistered-guests accounts. When balancing the bank deposit, the amount obtained must match the actual amounts collected in cash, checks, and credit card payments. The basic daily night auditing process can be summarized thus:

Opening balance (yesterday's outstanding balance) + Charges − Credits = Net outstanding (closing) balance

---

SITUATION 5.6   Night Audit Report

Anthony Padilla, a senior in a hotel and restaurant management program, is interviewing for a management-training job with the Sheraton Corporation. His first meeting on campus went well and he was invited to a second interview at company headquarters. After answering questions asked by a panel of corporate staff members, he is told that there is a position open as night auditor at a corporate property in Denver. This job would be a first step toward becoming front desk manager in the near future. To test Anthony's knowledge of night auditing, he is asked to solve a case related to balancing the night audit report. He is given the following categories and amounts:

Today's total revenue	$24,854.44
Today's write-offs, paid outs, and discounts	763.03
Today's cash revenue	11,514.39
Yesterday's outstanding balance	62,848.99
Today's credit card payments	17,041.61
Today's cash payments	18,393.75

ASSIGNMENT: You have been asked to help Anthony Padilla work out the following:

1. Today's credit revenue
2. Today's ending balance
3. Today's total bank deposit

KEY CONCEPTS/TERMS

balancing up	no-show
cancellation	opening balance
city ledger	opening team
closing balance	overbooking
cost based rate	overstay
direct bill	reservations bucket
executive committee	return on investment (ROI)
guest folio	understay
guest ledger	walking a guest
market based rate	yield management (YM)
meeting planner	

Chapter 6

Sales and Marketing Operations

CHAPTER OBJECTIVES

- Review how the analysis of a property and its surrounding area is conducted.
- Identify the property's business market segments.
- Determine the sales and marketing budget.
- Discuss how the target market segments can be reached.
- Write a letter of agreement.
- Understand how room revenue can be maximized by optimizing rack and group sales.

OVERVIEW

The hospitality industry offers a large selection of products to the public, ranging from guest rooms and food and beverage services to sophisticated convention packages that usually include concurrent meetings, exhibits, receptions, banquets, and recreational activities. In some cases, convention business can exceed 50 percent of the property's sales volume. Hospitality establishments, from the humble bed-and-breakfast operation to the megaresort, must develop a marketing program and a sales strategy that fulfill the needs of each property. In practice, the sales approach begins with the development of a marketing plan that includes the following basic components:

- *Analyses of the property and of the surrounding area (what is to be sold or where are we now).*
- *Identification of business segments or markets (who may be interested in the product the property offers).*

- *Calculation of financial resources needed to attract customers (how much the property is prepared to spend in the marketing effort).*
- *Ascertainment of ways to reach potential customers (how the advertising and promotional effort is going to be implemented).*

In other words, the sales department of a hospitality establishment must gather information about the property and the surrounding attractions in order to make objective marketing decisions. It will be difficult for a hotel, for example, to sell conventions if the property has a large convention hall but no breakout rooms—the small conference rooms used for meetings and other events. It will also be impossible to sell the concept of golfing if the nearest course is 50 miles away from the property and is accessible only by a circuitous, unpaved road.

Once the analyses are completed, the source of potential business must be identified. Should the establishment attempt to attract transient, group, convention, commercial, tour and travel, or banquet business from local, regional, national, and international markets? And how is the sales department going to attract these segments? By attending exhibitions and trade shows or by advertising in trade publications, magazines, radio, and newspaper? By direct mail? By direct contact? And how much would the marketing effort cost? In brief, marketing is all about finding out what potential guests want and providing them with the highest possible level of quality at reasonable cost in order to generate an acceptable profit.

Graduating seniors in hotel and restaurant management programs often want to be hired in the sales and marketing department of hospitality operations because of the glamour of going around dressed in expensive business attire entertaining potential customers. The fact is that their desire to begin their careers in sales and marketing is well founded. Having such a background provides excellent experience for future promotion to upper management. Companies understand that the success of hospitality operations is ultimately based on maximizing guest room occupancy and food and beverage sales.

ANALYSIS OF THE PROPERTY AND SURROUNDING AREA

In order to promote their product, the sales and marketing staff must be objective in listing the facilities, services, and activities the property can provide, and at the same time ascertaining whether their quality compares favorably or unfavorably with the establishment's direct competition. Hopefully, the property will be able to market some product or services unique to the market environment. The analysis will serve as a basis for the advertising and promotional campaign that must be implemented to sell the product.

SITUATION 6.1   Analysis of a Property in the Southwestern United States*

Alyse Rossi is a graduate from a 4-year hotel and restaurant management program. Her last 2 years in the industry have been as a sales associate with a nationwide hotel chain with headquarters in the Northwest. Wishing to move up on her career ladder, Alyse has accepted the position of director of sales with the Enchantment Resort in Sedona, Arizona. Being new to the property and to the local environment, Alyse decides to conduct a thorough analysis of the resort and its surrounding area. She begins with a list of specific questions:

What facilities and services does the resort offer guests?

What activities does the property advertise?

What are the natural and historical attractions of the surrounding area?

How do the climatic seasons of the Sedona area affect occupancy?

What is the competition, and does the Enchantment have an edge over existing establishments in the area?

What are the tourism counts and visitor profiles for the area?

ASSIGNMENT: Prepare an analysis of the Enchantment Resort in Sedona using information from the Hotel Travel Index, the property's Web site at www.enchantmentresort.com, the city of Sedona at www.sedonaguide.com and the Arizona Office of Tourism at www.arizonaguide.com.

*This analysis can be conducted on any other property preferred by instructors or students.

IDENTIFICATION OF BUSINESS MARKET SEGMENTS

Once the analyses of the property and surrounding areas have been completed, the sales office must define all possible sources of potential business. This step is critical to targeting the promotion efforts. Potential guests may have a wide range of reasons for wanting to stay at one establishment in particular; consideration must be given to the major urban centers in the area or to specific countries that have been or have the potential to be good business sources. For example, the largest number of European tourists to visit Arizona in the 1990s was from Germany. Other considerations to be weighed are natural attractions, significant cultural enclaves, and major historical sites that are within range of the property. For instance, an establishment that is near the Gettysburg battlefield will have excellent possibilities of attracting national and international history buffs.

The sales and marketing staff might pursue several possible sources of business:

- Business guests
- Leisure guests
- Transient and independent guests
- Independent and group tourists
- Conventions, conferences, and business gatherings
- Catered functions and banquets
- Organized tours

Special market subsegment trends present in specific environments should also be considered so that no potential source of business is overlooked. For instance, **special-interest travelers**—visitors interested in a specific tourism offer on attraction—may be looking for outdoor activities such as mountain biking, bird watching, or wildlife photography; **older travelers**—the segment of the industry comprised of senior citizens—usually prefer cultural and heritage attractions, Elderhostel educational trips, or guided nature tours; **weekend travelers** represent a market segment that may be attracted by value-for-dollar family packages or child-oriented activities; **nature tourism** involves those interested in natural attractions, ecotourism trips, or trekking.

SITUATION 6.2   Identifying Market Segments

After thoroughly analyzing the facilities and services of the Enchantment Resort and the attractions of the surrounding areas, Alyse Rossi decides to identify the local, regional, national, and international market segments and subsegments that could be targeted by the sales department.

ASSIGNMENT: Based on the analyses conducted, identify the market segments and areas of origin of potential customers who might be attracted to the Enchantment Resort. Present a written statement giving the reason why these market segments are attracted to this establishment.

DETERMINING THE SALES AND MARKETING BUDGET

The financial resources to be spent annually on sales and marketing efforts usually are a function of the projected revenues. Generally, more resources are needed when a product is introduced or relaunched than when a product already has its own place in the market. For example, although the typical revenue percentage allocated to the sales department is usually between 5 and 6 percent of the establishment's total revenue, it is not uncommon to allocate a much higher percentage if the property needs to start an intense campaign to advertise the product to new markets.

The typical yearly departmental expenses aimed at building rooms and food and beverage sales may include the following categories:

- Salaries and wages
- Direct-mail advertising
- Advertising directory
- Advertising literature
- Media and sign advertising
- Entertainment and promotion
- Travel expenses

As with other departments in the property, the sales and marketing director must present the budget to the general manager for approval.

SITUATION 6.3   Setting the Sales and Marketing Budget

After determining the market segments to be targeted, Alyse Rossi started working on the upcoming fiscal year's budget. She based her calculations on last year's figures, adding increases for several marketing initiatives that she had planned to implement. Specifically, Alyse plans to rent space for a highway sign on Interstate 17, to conduct a **sales blitz** in the cities of Phoenix and Tucson, to man a booth at the Tourism Fair in Berlin, Germany, and to invite tour operators to conduct on-site inspection visits. Alyse also has decided to add a new sales representative to her staff, bringing the total payroll and related expenses to $126,500. Next year's projected revenue is $6,325,000. She finds the existing advertising literature appropriate but has decided to have the property's Web site substantially updated.

Alyse worked out a comparison between last year's and next year's expense percentages that looks like this:

		Last Year		Next Year
Advertising literature	from	0.2%	to	0.6%
Advertising directory	from	0.2%	to	0.2%
Media and sign advertising	from	0.6%	to	0.8%
Entertainment and promotion	from	0.2%	to	0.6%
Travel expenses	from	0.1%	to	0.5%
Other expenses	from	0.4%	to	0.4%

ASSIGNMENT: Prepare a sales and marketing budget to be presented to the general manager for approval. All budget items must be justified with detailed explanations of planned expenses by category.

REACHING THE TARGET MARKET SEGMENTS

Once the environmental analysis is complete and the budget set, the typical marketing plan addresses the opportunities, strategies, and tactics to reach the market segments identified as "potential customers." Generally, individual guests can be attracted by way of the Internet, print-media campaigns, and sign and media advertising; convention and group business may be secured through direct mail or contact with government agencies, civic organizations, and professional, religious and nonprofit organizations as well as **meeting planners**—consultants employed by corporations to book conventions and other functions. Tourists, tour groups, and international travelers may be reached through tour operators, travel agents, and information presented at tourism exhibitions and trade shows. Weekend and family business can usually be attracted by **packaging**—combining rooms and complementary or discounted services into a single-price offering. Local and regional market segments can be reached by **personal selling**—sales efforts conducted either by telephone or face-to-face (**field sales**). **Inside sales** can be promoted by **suggestive selling** and **upselling** or by the **merchandising** of products. The sales function can also be increased by **publicity**—a nonpaid communication or information effort about the property by way of **news releases** and **press conferences**.

SITUATION 6.4   Sales Implementation

The next task to be accomplished by Alyse Rossi is to develop an implementation plan describing how the identified target areas—potential business sources—are to be reached. In practice, the implementation should be presented in detail to the property's general manager together with a sequential, chronological, and detailed advertising schedule.

ASSIGNMENT: Prepare detailed advertising and promotional efforts to sell guest rooms and food and beverage functions as previously identified.

THE LETTER OF AGREEMENT

A business sale often begins with the establishment receiving a query letter from a company or other entity stating the needs to be fulfilled by the property, such as dates, number of rooms and meeting space required, meal functions, and billing procedure. The sales department must respond promptly to the request with a proposal stating prices, terms, and general conditions. If accepted and signed, this becomes the **letter of agreement**—the formal acceptance by the two parties to go ahead with the business deal. Serving as a contract between the two parties, the letter should be clearly written and all matters related to the upcoming event adequately itemized. Nothing should be left to verbal arrangement so there is no misunderstanding regarding the function or billing procedures.

SITUATION 6.5   Preparing a Letter of Agreement

You are the sales manager of a convention hotel in Houston, Texas. The Nestle Purina Company has decided to hold a convention in your hotel from August 15 through August 18, and they are requesting a confirmation. You have checked meeting space and room availability for the period of the stay and found that you can accommodate their needs. You are prepared to provide the following services:

Guest Rooms

> 200 double rooms for single or double occupancy
>
> 1 **junior suite** for the regional manager
>
> 1 **hospitality suite** to be used for entertaining company members

Guests Check In and Out

> Some guests will be arriving one day before the official beginning of the convention but most attendees are due the evening of August 15, departing the morning of August 18.
>
> The company requests complimentary shuttle from the airport to the hotel between 4 PM to 11 PM and from hotel to airport between 7 AM and 2 PM.
>
> Purina requests **preregistration** of all guests.

Billing Procedures

> Flat rate of $130 per room for single or double occupancy to be paid directly by guests.
>
> Complimentary junior suite.
>
> A discount of 50 percent on **rack rate** for the hospitality suite.
>
> General meeting room charge: $1,500 per day.
>
> **Breakout rooms** at $300 each per day.
>
> **Direct bill** of **master account** for all meal functions, **incidental charges** of the presidential suite, and room charge for the hospitality suite and meeting rooms.

Meeting Rooms

Theater-style room setup in general meeting room, for 300 people on August 16 and 17 with podium and **standing mike** plus one **roving mike**.

E-shaped room setup for four 50-person breakout rooms for the same dates, with stands for **flip charts** and overhead projectors.

Meal Functions

Continental breakfast on August 16 and 17 at $3.95 and lunch at $8.25 per person.

Dinner on August 17 at $16.50 per person and **host bar** at $3.75 per ticket filled (2 per person). A 24-hour guarantee is required for lunch and dinner. The **room setup** will be 5 percent over guarantee.

Gratuities

The total of all services to be surcharged 15 percent for gratuities.

ASSIGNMENT: Prepare a letter of agreement to be sent in duplicate, asking Purina to return a signed copy. Be sure to address the following items:

1. Confirmation of dates
2. Confirmation of guest room and meeting room arrangement
3. **Cutoff date** for guest rooms
4. Confirmation of arrival pattern and transfer
5. Confirmation of meal functions and liquor service
6. Confirmation of billing procedure and method of payment
7. Inclusion of a clause in case either party is forced to cancel because of circumstances beyond its control.
8. Statement of gratuities and city and state tax charges to be added to the bill

SITUATION 6.6   Ascertaining the Package Price

After receiving the letter of agreement, the meeting planner at Purina decides to consider picking up the cost of the guest rooms if the total bill is within the allocated budget expenses for the convention. To this effect, the hotel received a request to work out the price per person per night in single and double occupancy. Purina is ready to pay $115 per room per night for single occupancy and $65 per person per night for double occupancy. The price of the meals stays the same. Purina now wants to add two refreshment breaks on August 16 and

17 at $1.75 per person and reduce the host bar tickets to one per person. They also want to know the price per **day guest** including lunch, and the two refreshment breaks only.

ASSIGNMENT: Calculate the price per person per night for single and double occupancy and the price per day guest.

MAXIMIZING ROOM REVENUE

Although filling a property at rack rate prices is ideal, most large establishments must rely on group business to fill the house, particularly during the **shoulder season** or **low season**. The rationale is that it is better to have rooms occupied at discounted rates than to have them empty. However, when the demand for guest rooms is there, it is the job of the sales department to give preference to transient and individual guests who pay full price rather than to groups that generally receive substantial discounts. On the other hand, sometimes it is preferable to accept a convention, even if the transient demand is high, in order not to lose that particular piece of business in the future. Generally, the rule of thumb for sales managers is to level out the valleys in room occupancy by booking group business.

SITUATION 6.7   Balancing Rack Rate and Discounted Group Business Occupancy

Max Gonzalez has been promoted to sales director of a resort and spa establishment south of Pittsburgh. The date is January 10. Max has received three requests for group business for the second week of October:

> The Friends of the Earth, an ecological organization with headquarters in Philadelphia, wants to book the resort's 280 rooms from Monday, October 7, through Thursday, October 11. They are willing to contract for a flat rate of $110 per room per night.
>
> The Shriners wish to reserve 40 percent of the hotel capacity. The group would arrive Monday, October 6, and depart Thursday, October 9. They could pay a flat rate per room of $135 per night.
>
> The Republican Women wish to book 50 percent of the resort's room capacity at $125 flat rate per room. Their stay is from Tuesday, October 8, to Friday, October 11.

Max has been asked by the general manager to work out the optimum revenue from rooms that the resort can achieve during the second week in October, taking into consideration the number of rooms and rates that the groups require and the occupancy trends of the property for the week in question for the last 5 years. Max looks up the historical records of the resort and finds the following:

Daily Minimum Room Occupancy Percentages for the Last 5 Years During the Second Week in October (Monday Through Friday)

Transient and individual occupancy (rack rates)	50%
Corporate, government and other discounted occupancy	10%

Current ADR

Rack rates	$150
Corporate, government, and other discounted rates	135

ASSIGNMENT: Which group should the resort accept to maximize room revenue? (Note that you should not take into account the potential F&B business.)

KEY CONCEPTS/TERMS

breakout room
cutoff date
day guest
direct bill
E-shaped room setup
field sales
flip chart
hospitality suite
host bar
incidental charges
inside sales
junior suite
letter of agreement
low season
master account
meeting planner
merchandising
nature tourism

news release
older travelers
packaging
personal selling
preregistration
press conference
publicity
rack rate
room setup
roving mike
sales blitz
shoulder season
special-interest traveler
standing mike
suggestive selling
theater-style room setup
upselling
weekend traveler

Chapter 7

Engineering Operations

CHAPTER OBJECTIVES

- Review the engineering department budget.
- Discuss water supply to hospitality operations, water charges, and water conservation.
- Discuss the details of electricity management, electricity charges, and electricity conservation.
- Understand the basic concepts of building heating management and natural gas charges.
- Discuss the details of air-conditioning management and energy conservation.

OVERVIEW

The teaching of engineering and maintenance functions is not widespread in college hospitality programs. Although some institutions teach this course in depth, others skim over it, combine it with other courses, or do not teach it at all. There are two reasons for this oversight: one is that some curriculum decision makers believe that in practice, engineering and maintenance in hospitality operations is always left to experts in the field (not to hospitality graduates); the other is that this subject is not an easy one to teach, and it is thus preferable to leave it out of the program. Nevertheless, students from hospitality programs should possess a basic knowledge of engineering and maintenance operations at the time of graduation because, at some time in their careers, plant managers and maintenance supervisors will be reporting to them matters related to facilities management. It is also important for managers to know ways to maximize energy conservation.

DETERMINING THE ENGINEERING BUDGET

The financial resources allocated to the engineering department depend greatly on factors such as the age and physical state of the property, the cost of energy in the area where the establishment is located, the degree of maintenance performed on the building and equipment in the past, and the property's levels of occupancy.

The items of an engineering budget can be divided into three categories: (1) payroll and related expenses, (2) energy, and (3) operating and maintenance expenses. As a nonrevenue-producing department, engineering does not generate any income; the expense percentages, however, are a function of the establishment's total revenue. The total cost of the department's budget usually adds up to around 10 percent of total revenue depending, as stated before, on several factors. For example, a 40-year-old hotel usually requires more maintenance than one that has been built recently. A resort whose installations have been neglected over a period of time will probably need more effort and resources to maintain equipment than an establishment whose upkeep has been ongoing and thorough.

The category of "energy" usually includes payments to utility companies for the following:

- Electricity
- Gas and fuel
- Water and sewage

Property operations usually include items such as the following:

- Supplies for building repairs and maintenance
- Supplies for HVAC repairs and maintenance
- Supplies for plumbing and heating repairs and maintenance
- Pest control
- Trash removal
- Swimming pool supplies, repairs, and maintenance
- Grounds and landscaping repairs and maintenance

The engineering budget is generally compiled taking the department's past year performance (previous budget results) as a guideline, and factors such as predicted fluctuations on energy prices, the implementation of energy conservation programs, refurbishing projects, and occupancy projections. As with other departments in the property, the plant manager (chief engineer) must present the proposed budget to management for its approval.

SITUATION 7.1 Supervising the Engineering Budget

Megan Dykstra has been promoted to assistant general manager of a 487-room hotel in Pittsburgh. One of Megan's many responsibilities is that of overseeing the activities of the engineering department. Although the plant manager is an experienced professional with 8 years work with the company, he has the reputation of padding his department's budget in order to "cover himself" at the end of the fiscal year. Megan has been asked by the property's general manager to have next year's engineering budget adjusted down to real expectations. Specifically, the plant manager must take into account the following factors:

1. The price of gas and fuel is expected to go up by 3 percent.
2. The price of electricity is expected to go down by 2 percent.
3. The effect of this year's conservation program implemented throughout the building is expected to reduce water consumption by 6 percent. Water charges are expected to remain unchanged.
4. The elimination of one maintenance employee will provide a combined savings of $38,000 to the category for payroll and related expenses. There will not be any pay raises in the department next year.
5. The establishment's predicted occupancy will remain the same as last year's.
6. No special repairs have been scheduled for next year.
7. The estimated total revenue for next year is $8,571,540.

Armed with this information, Megan carefully studied the first draft of next year's budget presented to her by the plant manager. Immediately, she noticed that the cost percentages were exactly the same as those in last year's budget.

	Last Year's Percentages	Plant Engineer's	
		Budget Draft	Percentages
Payroll and related	2.2	$188,574	2.2
Electricity	2.1	180,002	2.1
Gas and fuel	0.8	68,572	0.8
Water and sewage	0.4	34,286	0.4
Property operations	2.8	240,003	2.8

ASSIGNMENT: Redo next year's engineering budget to reflect the factors that the plant engineer should have considered before presenting the draft. Megan asked the plant engineer to reduce the total cost by $41,600. Was she right?

WATER SUPPLY MANAGEMENT

The water supply to most hospitality operations in the United States is provided by a public utility. It is up to the provider company to supply potable water and maintain a sanitary sewage system. In the case of properties away from urban centers, it is the responsibility of the operators to treat the water so that it is safe for human consumption.

Common problems with the water supply include lack of sufficient, constant pressure of the water flow, water hardness, and noise from plumbing vibration. The installation of water pumps, water softeners, and piping loops and expansion joints can take care of these deficiencies. In practice, operational problems caused by flaws in the water supply system are addressed by the plant manager for technical solutions.

As the country's water resources continue to diminish, most utility companies keep increasing water charges in an effort to limit consumption. Graduates from hotel and restaurant management programs should join the industry with a clear understanding about water and sewerage charges, and water conservation.

Water and Sewerage Charges

Generally, hospitality properties are assessed a **basic charge**—a minimum amount charged regardless of consumption. Water consumption is often billed based on levels of water consumed; that is, an establishment may have to pay higher rates if the consumption is over preestablished thresholds. For example, for residential accounts the city of Flagstaff, Arizona, charges $2.83 per 1,000 gallons for the first 5,000 gallons consumed, and $4.71 per 1,000 gallons for consumption over 15,000 gallons. Wastewater is charged at $2.73 per 1,000 gallons.

SITUATION 7.2   Calculation of Water and Wastewater Charges

As assistant manager of a resort in the Midwest, you have been asked to forecast the cost of the property's potable water and wastewater for the month of June. After reviewing historical records and occupancy percentages, you calculate that the resort will consume 300,000 gallons for the month. The utility company provides you with the following information:

Service charge for an 8-inch meter size	$124.00
Charge for the first 50,000 gallons	2.83 per 1,000 gallons
Charge for the next 100,000 gallons	3.32 per 1,000 gallons
Charge for more than 150,000 gallons	4.71 per 1,000 gallons
Charge per 1,000 gallons for 100 percent of waste water	3.58

ASSIGNMENT: Based on the water and sewage charges billed by the utility and the forecasted water consumption, work out an estimate cost for June.

Water Conservation

Because dripping valves and faucets do increase water costs, leakages should be repaired as soon as they are detected. To emphasize the cost to the property of water losses, let us assume that each day there are on average 10 dripping faucets in a hotel. If each faucet loses 3 gallons of water per day, the establishment will have lost 10,950 gallons of water annually ($3 \times 10 \times 365$). In the case of running toilets, the number of gallons lost per year can be much higher. The cost of leaking hot-water faucets is compounded by the energy spent and Btu's used to heat the constantly running water.

Besides preventing water leakages and repairing faucets and toilets as soon as problems are discovered, water costs can be lowered by using low-flow shower heads and low water-consumption toilets or by adjusting the toilet vacuum flush mechanisms. Ideally, toilets should not use more than 3 gallons of water per flush and shower heads, on average, should consume about 2.5 gallons per minute.

SITUATION 7.3   Minimizing Water Usage

John Harvey has been appointed assistant to the general manager of a busy downtown hotel in southern California. In addition to his normal duties, he has been assigned the special project of lowering the cost paid for water by suggesting ways to conserve consumption. The property general manager's comments were that the bill had been steadily increasing for the past 3 years in spite of the fact that charges by the utility company had not been raised and that hotel occupancy had been steady.

John started by conducting a thorough, systematic, month-long **walking survey**—an inspection of the building conducted on site. John's findings were as follows:

> Average number of faucets found dripping daily in the 30-day period: 35; estimated water loss per faucet: 3 gallons per day.
>
> Average number of toilet **ghost flush** found: 16; estimated water loss per toilet: 16 gallons per day.
>
> Water per flush for each guestroom toilet: 6 gallons.

In addition, all shower heads had been retrofitted 5 years ago with **flow controllers** to minimize consumption. John knew that the 450-room hotel was running at 78 percent occupancy annually and that the average person per occupied room was 1.45. He arbitrarily assigned an average of four flushes per person per day for toilet use. John's plan consisted of starting a program to change valve seat washers of dripping faucets as soon as they were reported to maintenance, hoping to reduce the daily average number of leaks from 35 to 6. In addition, John planned to reduce the number of ghost-flushing toilets to a maximum of 6 per day. He also proposed to adjust the vacuum flush mechanisms of all toilets to reduce the gallons of water per flush from 6 to 3.5 in all guest rooms.

ASSIGNMENT: Present a water consumption reduction proposal to the general manager of the hotel indicating the number of gallons of water that would be saved annually if John's plan were adopted by management.

ELECTRICITY MANAGEMENT

Electric energy was relatively inexpensive in the United States until the 1970s. As a result, American consumers developed a tendency to be extravagant with electricity consumption, a trend that in most cases is still prevalent today. The average hospitality industry establishment may very well spend 3 percent of its total revenue to pay for electricity consumption alone. Since the energy crisis of the late 1990s, particularly after the rolling blackouts in California, there has been an increasing need to manage energy costs effectively. As a consequence, students in hotel and restaurant management programs must have an in-depth understanding of the negative impact that energy costs can have on an operation's bottom line. It is important for hospitality graduates to bring to the industry ideas and techniques to curb electricity consumption.

Electricity Charges

Electricity is measured in **hertz**—a unit of measurement of current or sound vibrations per second. In most cases it is provided by utility companies in single or three-phase (60 hertz) standard **voltage**. Three-phase service is generally furnished for motors of an individual rated capacity above 7 1/2 **horsepower (HP)**. The rates charged to hospitality companies vary by region. The formula used to calculate rates is complex and usually involves a basic charge as well as different rates based on the most **kilowatts (kW)** (1,000 watts) used in a 15-minute period (demand portion of the bill) and the total number of kilowatts consumed. In addition, rates may vary by season. In Arizona, for example, rates are higher during the summer billing cycle. Electric utilities may also have a bill surcharge for low **power factor**—the time at which volts supplied and **amperes** required reach their peak at maximum values. If they do not peak at the same time, and the power factor drops below a preset value, the utility company may impose a surcharge to be paid by the consumer.

The determination of kilowatts is thus ascertained by the average kilowatts supplied during the 15-minute period of maximum use during the month, as determined from readings of the meter. The **demand rate** is determined by the most kilowatts used in any 15-minute period during **on-peak hours** and by the most kilowatts used in any 15-minute period during **off-peak hours**. Charges are determined by multiplying kilowatt-hours (kWh) by the different rates imposed by the utility company.

SITUATION 7.4   Calculation of Electricity Charges

Let us consider a hypothetical situation in which a property in Tucson, Arizona, has to pay the following charges:

Basic rate	$12.50
Flat-rate off-peak kilowatt-hour	0.07098
Flat-rate on-peak kilowatt-hour	0.10359
On-peak demand charge per kilowatt-hour	4.991
Off-peak demand charge per kilowatt-hour	1.73
Preestablished power factor level	0.84

The consumption for the month was as follows:

Kilowatts consumed during on-peak hours	33,840
Kilowatts consumed during off-peak hours	18,420
Maximum kilowatt-hour demand on-peak	804
Maximum kilowatt-hour demand off-peak	642
Minimum on-peak power factor recorded	0.82
Minimum off-peak power factor recorded	0.69

ASSIGNMENT: Calculate the total charge for the electricity consumed by the property, keeping in mind that the power factor charge is computed on the maximum kilowatt-hour demand on-peak and off-peak at the rates of $4.991 and $1.73 per kWh.

Electricity Conservation

Increasing energy costs and impending shortages are compelling reasons for hospitality establishments to conserve energy. Reducing wasted guest room electricity by 30 to 50 percent can be achieved by installing wireless passive infrared people detectors and door sensors. These devices are capable of noticing whether or not a guest room is occupied and of providing customized climate control. For example, at $0.08 kWh, a 275-watt television set, left on needlessly for 2 hours per day will cost approximately $50 per year. One 2000-watt coffeemaker can cost the property $275 annually if left on for 4 hours per day. Four incandescent lightbulbs left on unnecessarily for 4 hours per day when a guest room is unoccupied will cost $50 per year.

The savings on electricity can be substantial if incandescent lightbulbs are replaced with compact fluorescent lamps. The latter use only about 25 percent of the energy required by incandescent bulbs while providing the same quality of light. Besides, fluorescent bulbs last about ten times longer than incandescent. Other ways to save electricity is by scheduling consumption (laundry and baking operations, for instance) during off-peak hours.

SITUATION 7.5   Minimizing Electricity Consumption

Claire Takinen the new assistant manager of a hotel in Tucson, Arizona, has been asked to determine the consumption and replacement costs of the 450, 75-watt incandescent lightbulbs currently in use in the hotel's guest room hallways with compact fluorescent lightbulbs. The internal corridors require that the lightbulbs are switched on 24 hours a day. The current average cost of each kilowatt-hour paid by the property is $0.09331.

ASSIGNMENT: If the cost of 1 fluorescent lightbulb is $1.90 and its wattage is 60, how many days will be necessary to amortize the purchase cost of the new lightbulbs from the savings obtained by lowering the bulbs' wattage? Claire is not considering the cost of replacing the lightbulbs and the effect of the life of both bulb types.

BUILDING HEATING MANAGEMENT

The most common building heating fuel sources used by hospitality companies are electricity, oil, and natural gas. Electric heating can be delivered by passing electricity through a **resistance** that becomes red hot, radiating the heat into the space to be heated. Air-conditioned **decentralized systems** can also deliver heating by way of a **heat pump**, a device that uses the refrigeration cycle to provide heat. This is achieved by reversing the direction of the functions of the evaporator and condenser components of the system. The use of electricity as a source for building heating is usually expensive.

Oil is used to generate building heat by burning it in a **furnace**, a structure in which to generate hot air, or in a **boiler**, a closed vessel in which to generate hot water or steam. The hot air is driven by fans through a **duct**, a conduit through which air is circulated, and the hot water or steam passes through pipes. The burning of oil to generate heat may cause discharges of harmful gases into the environment. Using oil as a heating resource also requires frequent checks for proper combustion and regular maintenance to keep the burners clean.

Natural gas is perhaps the best type of fuel for building heating as it is clean burning, requires limited maintenance, and is usually less costly than electricity. Centralized systems that use natural gas to generate warm air are the most common and effective heat-distribution systems in hospitality operations.

Natural Gas Charges

Utility companies use several methods to charge for gas consumption. Monthly charges are based on the use of the **therm**—a unit equal to 100,000 Btu. Some utility companies apply different rates according to the levels of therms used; others charge the same rate to the total number of therms consumed. There is always a customer charge per meter per month regardless of the amount of gas used.

SITUATION 7.6   Calculation of Natural Gas Charges

Based on the monthly basic cost of service rates shown below, predict the total cost (before tax), assuming that the gas used by a hotel during March was 12,500 therms:

Charge per meter	$18.00
First 500 therms, per therm	1.76
Next 500 therms, per therm	0.9267
Next 5,000 therms, per therm	0.6827
Next 5,000 therms, per therm	0.5794
Over 11,000 therms, per therm	0.5094

ASSIGNMENT: Predict gas usage cost for this property for March.

AIR-CONDITIONING MANAGEMENT

As with heating, air conditioning can be provided in decentralized systems by a heat pump that uses a closed circuit in which a **compressor** causes the **coolant gas** to condense and become frigid. The chilled gas is circulated into a **coil**, a continuous pipe forming spirals or rings through which space air is forced by way of a fan. This process causes the space air to cool while the refrigerant gas becomes warm and expands. The gas is again recirculated to the compressor and condenser where it is chilled again.

Most large hospitality operations use centralized systems in which water is the refrigerant. **Water-cooling towers**—an additional way of cooling the refrigerant water—can be used in conjunction with these systems. Once the water is chilled, it is piped into individual guest room coils where it comes in contact with space air, causing it to cool.

Heat and Air-Conditioning Conservation

The operation and maintenance of energy-generating systems is the responsibility of the engineering department personnel, who are experts in their fields.

The conservation of energy, however, is the responsibility of the property's management. Graduates from hotel and restaurant management programs must be aware that overconsumption of energy has a negative impact on the financial bottom line—in addition to depleting our planet's resources.

Managers can prevent the loss of heated or cooled air by training employees to keep thermostats at the right temperature, by installing computer-based people sensors in guest rooms that deactivate heating and cooling units when no one is in the rooms, by reducing ventilation by exhaust fans, and by minimizing heat or cool air losses. Opening kitchen and laundry room doors, for example, will allow large amounts of heat to "invade" refrigerated areas in summer.

Heat transfer is a process that occurs when a difference of temperature exists between two spaces. If the loss of heat or conditioned air is substantial, the amount of energy required to keep the temperature at comfortable levels has to be increased. In addition to the physical ways to minimize an air-conditioned loss—from maintaining thermostats at adequate levels to keeping doors closed—hospitality operators can reduce heat transfer by improving building insulation. For example, a single-glass windowpane will allow more heat to infiltrate or escape the building than a double-glass pane; similarly 12 inches of insulation in the attic will be more energy-efficient than 8 inches.

A **heat-transmission coefficient** provides a way of measuring the capability of any type of insulation (glass, walls, ceilings). It is measured in Btu per hour per square foot in degrees Fahrenheit. The better the insulated medium is, the lower the heat transmission coefficient will be. Situation 7.7 illustrates the relationship between heat transfer and the heat-transmission coefficient.

SITUATION 7.7 Heat and Air-conditioning Conservation

Natalia Gomez, general manager of a resort in Des Moines, Iowa, was asked by her corporate office supervisor to lower energy costs during the coming winter. Natalia decided to put into effect all energy-conservation techniques learned in her hospitality engineering class. She began by finding out how many Btu's per hour could be saved by upgrading the glass windows in the resort's dining room. She decided to apply the formula recommended by her engineering professor to determine insulation results:

$$T = SA \times C \, (t_i - t_o)$$

where T = heat transfer in Btu per hour

SA = area in square feet of the surface considered

C = heat transmission coefficient of insulator

t_i = inside temperature

t_o = outside temperature

Natalia considered changing the four single-pane, 10 × 15 ft dining room windows with a heat transmission coefficient of 1.13 with insulating double-pane glass having a 0.65 coefficient. She learned from the local weather bureau that the maximum temperature in Des Moines for the month of March was 46 and the minimum was 33. For her calculations, she assigned an average daily temperature of 40 degrees Fahrenheit.

ASSIGNMENT: How many Btu's per hour would be saved by changing the windows to the new specifications while maintaining the inside temperature at 69 degrees Fahrenheit?

KEY CONCEPTS/TERMS

ampere	heat transfer
basic charge	heat-transmission coefficient
boiler	hertz
coil	horsepower (HP)
compressor	kilowatt (kW)
coolant gas	off-peak hours
decentralized system	on-peak hours
demand rate	power factor
duct	resistance
flow controller	therm
furnace	voltage
ghost flush	walking survey
heat pump	water-cooling tower

Chapter 8

Controlling Hospitality Operations

CHAPTER OBJECTIVES

- Review the concept of the control function in management.
- Practice budgeting procedures for restaurants and lodging departments.
- Explain the format and purpose of profit and loss (P&L) statements.
- Work out a variance analysis exercise.
- Describe physical inventories and inventory turnover.
- Resolve a situational case of food cost reconciliation.

OVERVIEW

The control of resources in hospitality operations is achieved by way of budgets, inventories, and accounting procedures. Operating budgets are used to forecast sales, expenses, and profits and to limit operating costs to predetermined percentages of the projected revenues. Operational controls take effect when financial statements providing data on how the firm is performing are analyzed and interpreted by management. Two important operational statements are generated during the course of the fiscal year: the profit and loss statement (P&L) and the variance analysis.

Regular physical inventories are necessary to ascertain the cost percentages of merchandise used in a certain period of time, to figure out quantities of products needed to restock departments, and to find out if losses (pilferage) of items have occurred.

Ascertaining the food and beverage cost percentages is of critical importance in restaurant and lodging operations. The results will determine whether or not the money spent to prepare food and to serve drinks yields a sufficient gross house profit to cover other operational and management costs and to generate an adequate return on investment. The calculation of food and beverage cost per-centages can be quite complex, particularly in establishments with several food and beverage outlets subject to many variable factors such as inventories, purchases, products issued, spoilage, and interdepartmental credits.

The control-of-operations function in hospitality establishments must be un-derstood fully by graduates. Regardless of the size of the operation, it is central to the organization's management policy—especially for establishing goals, analyzing results, and taking corrective actions if necessary.

THE CONTROL FUNCTION

Hospitality line managers must regularly assess the operational performance of their units or departments against preestablished forecasts and standards usu-ally set by upper management. The purpose of this assessment is to find out how well (or how badly) the unit or department has done operationally and to redi-rect efforts to optimize future results. Young supervisors and managers should make themselves acquainted, as soon as they are hired, with the computer pro-grams (usually state-of-the-art) used in their place of employment. However, regardless of their understanding of the mechanics of report feedback newly hired graduates should have a clear understanding of why and how the control function must be exerted; that is, point of sale (POS) and accounting systems endowed with highly complex software should be seen only as helpful control-ling tools, not as miraculous problem-solving devices.

Budgeting

There are several kinds of budgets, although the types that will be encountered by entry-level hospitality graduates are **short-term**—usually one-year (month by month), restaurant budgets and departmental budgets in lodging establish-ments. Typically, every department of a property prepares a budget for the up-coming **fiscal year** that includes the projected revenue, the estimated operating expenses, and the anticipated departmental income. Departments that are not revenue-generating, such as engineering, only forecast their operating expenses. The amounts for the revenue and expense categories must be justified, both quantitatively and in narrative. The most common departmental budgets in lodging operations are the F&B and rooms division budgets.

RESTAURANT BUDGETS

There are a number of operational budgets used by restaurants. The **fixed budget** is based on only one level of sales. The annual budget should be broken down by month, because business usually goes up and down and is influenced by factors such as seasons, special events, economic factors, and the competition. The an-nual budget represents the sum of amounts for the 12 months of the year.

Annual revenue projections are generally calculated from past revenue figures, the state of the local economy, and competition pressures, such as a new restaurant being built nearby. Restaurant expenses are worked out as percentages of sales, keeping in mind that there may be internal and external factors affecting the costs. For example, the amount allocated to salaries and wages will have to be increased if an extra line cook is added in the kitchen or if the federal government increases the minimum wage.

Typically, a restaurant budget consists of **food revenue** and **beverage revenue**; the **cost of sales** for both food and beverage; **operating expenses**, and **occupancy costs**. Total revenue minus the cost of sales equals the restaurant's **gross profit**. Gross profit minus operating expenses equals the **profit before occupancy costs**. **Income** (profit) is the result of subtracting occupancy costs from the profit before occupancy costs.

SITUATION 8.1   Improving the Annual Fixed Budget of a Restaurant

Anthony Ponti has been hired by an independent family restaurant as manager. The owner contacted Anthony because he was a graduate of a hotel and restaurant management program and had 2 years industry experience with a nationwide restaurant chain. Anthony has been given permission to "change things around" in order to improve the establishment's bottom line. The restaurant's fixed budget last year showed the following figures:

	Dollars	Percentage
Sales		
Food	894,600	94.0
Beverage	55,200	6.0
	949,800	100.0
Cost of Sales		
Food	304,164	34.0
Beverage	14,904	27.0
	319,068	34.0
Total Gross Profit	630,732	66.0
Operating Expenses		
Payroll and related expenses	294,438	31.0
Employee meals	14,247	1.5
Operating supplies	94,980	10.0
Administration and general	14,247	1.5
Advertising and promotion	18,996	2.0
Repairs and maintenance	18,996	2.0
Energy costs	37,992	4.0
Total Operating Expense	493,896	52.0
Profit Before Occupancy Costs	136,836	14.0
Occupancy costs	47,490	5.0
Income Before Taxes	89,346	9.0

Anthony performed a walking analysis of the property, perused all past records, and investigated the local market and the competition. He decided that there was a good chance to improve the overall performance of the restaurant by allocating additional funds to the advertising budget, improving customer service, and starting an aggressive merchandising program, which would greatly increase the number of covers sold. He also determined that the food cost percentage could be lowered by improving purchasing procedures (portion control and waste were being satisfactorily controlled by the chef). Anthony would also lower the beverage cost percentage by training bartenders and by changing the pouring system now in place to a more effective one. His improvement plan for the next fiscal year was as follows:

- Lower the food cost percentage from 34 to 28.
- Lower the beverage percentage from 27 to 25.
- Allocate an additional $2,000 per month to advertising and promotion.

He hoped these changes would have several effects:

- Increase food sales by 20 percent.
- Increase beverage sales by 20 percent.
- Increase payroll and related expenses by $2,500 per month.
- Increase operating supplies by $900 per month.
- Increase energy cost by $400 per month.

Anthony decided to maintain all other operating expense categories and occupancy costs at the current percentages of revenue.

ASSIGNMENT: Present a budget for the next fiscal year reflecting the changes proposed by Anthony, explaining the reasons for arriving at the new amounts. Give your own critique of the proposal, agreeing or disagreeing with Anthony's plan.

DEPARTMENTAL BUDGETS

Lodging operations must prepare **departmental budgets** in order to control the performance of each one of the departments that the property operates. The two most important departmental budgets are the rooms division and the food and beverage department budgets. As in restaurants, departmental budgets are broken down by month because the volume of business is, in most cases, not consistent throughout the year.

Rooms Division Budget

The income statement for the rooms division consists of the **estimated revenue** from selling guest rooms, minus the **estimated direct expenses** for the division. The estimated revenue is calculated month by month by multiplying the number of guest rooms projected to be sold by the estimated average daily rate (ADR). The estimated direct operating expenses include those of the house-keeping and front office departments. The structure of the rooms division budget usually is as follows:

> Revenue
> − Total payroll and related
> − Other expenses
> = Department profit

The payroll and related entry is usually broken down into front office salaries, housekeeping salaries, payroll taxes and employee relations, and employee meals. The other expenses include categories for costs incurred in by the front office and housekeeping departments. A typical front office cost is travel commissions (commissions paid to travel agents and tour operators for reservations made at the property); typical housekeeping costs include cleaning supplies, laundry supplies, and linen replacements. Other categories, such as uniforms and stationery supplies, may belong to both departments. As with all budgets, all amounts must be justified before the projections are approved by management.

SITUATION 8.2   Rooms Division Department Budget

As assistant to the rooms division director of a 300-room luxury resort in the San Diego area, you have been asked to prepare the **consolidated room sales statement**—the projection of room sales for the fiscal year. The first step is for you to consider the following factors:

- Past revenue figures and trends
- Current bookings and anticipated business trends
- Local, regional, and national economic factors
- Local competition
- Other circumstantial limiting factors

After weighing carefully all factors and trends, you come to the conclusion that the national economic growth as a whole has remained flat from last year. However, predictions indicate that the local economy will grow by 5 percent. The country's inflation is running at 2.5 percent. A new 500-room hotel has opened across the bay from Coronado Island that may influence bookings negatively during the coming year. You decide to keep the overall monthly occupancy percentages from last year while increasing last year's rates 2.5 percent to compete with the newly built hotel and compensate for inflation.

	Occupancy Percentage	ADR	Remarks
January	85	$225	
February	98	196	Boeing Corp. convention booked
March	82	214	
April	86	206	
May	78	206	
June	52	195	Remodeling of 80 guest rooms
July	50	194	Remodeling continues
August	78	201	End of remodeling
September	90	184	Technology convention booked
October	82	190	
November	85	195	
December	75	175	

ASSIGNMENT: Prepare the consolidated room sales and projected revenue. Calculate the total number of rooms sold, the average annual occupancy percentage, the average yearly ADR, and the total revenue projected for next year.

F&B Department Budget

The income statement for the F&B department consists of the estimated revenue from selling food, beverages, and other department revenue (such as room rentals) minus the cost of sales and the estimated direct expenses. The estimated revenue is calculated each month by multiplying the number of forecasted covers by the projected average check for both food *and* beverage. The revenue and salaries are usually calculated for each operating outlet. The structure of the F&B budget usually follows this pattern:

> Food revenue by outlet
> + Beverage revenue by outlet
> + Other income
> − Cost of sales for food *and* beverages
> = Gross profit
> − Salaries and wages by outlet
> − Payroll and related
> − Other expenses
> = Department profit

The payroll and related entry usually consists of payroll taxes and employee relations, and employee meals.

SITUATION 8.3   F&B Department Budget

Danielle Gee is the food and beverage manager of a 300-room property located near Denver's old Stapleton Airport. The hotel operates a restaurant (the Atrium), a lounge (Applause), and banquet/convention facilities. Danielle must prepare next year's budget for her department. After receiving information from F&B department heads, she is ready to prepare a budget, beginning with August, the first month of the fiscal year.

Food Revenue

Atrium	18,000 covers @ $5.52/average check
Room service	3,800 covers @ $6.75/average check
Banquets	5,950 covers @ $8.23/average check

Beverage Revenue

Applause Lounge	9,400 covers @ $4.25/average check
Atrium	$5,940
Room service	$3,420
Banquets	$6,426

Other Income

Room rentals	$7,950
Other	$3,700

Cost of Sales

Cost of food	33.8% (2 percentage points lower than last year)
Cost of beverage	22.9% (same percentage as last year)

Salaries and Wages

Atrium salaries	21.5% (0.5 percentage point lower than last year)
Room service salaries	23.4% (3 percentage points higher than last year)
Banquet salaries	9.8% (same percentage as last year)
Applause salaries	15.2% (same percentage as last year)
Kitchen salaries	14.3% (2 percentage points lower than last year)
F&B management salaries	2.1% (0.5 percentage point higher than last year)

Payroll Taxes and Benefits	8.5% (0.2 percentage point higher than last year)

Other Expenses

Outside services	0.7% (same percentage as last year)
Cleaning supplies	0.5% (same percentage as last year)
Napery	0.7% (0.5 percentage point higher than last year)
Guest supplies	0.2% (same percentage as last year)
China, glass, and silver	0.3% (0.2 percentage point lower than last year)
Music and entertainment	1.2% (same percentage as last year)
Printing and stationery	0.3% (same percentage as last year)
Uniforms	0.5% (0.3 percentage points higher than last year)
Paper supplies	0.1% (0.2 percentage point lower than last year)
Incentives	0.2% (same percentage as last year)

ASSIGNMENT: Using the appropriate format, work out the gross profit and projected income in dollars as well as the percentage, for the month of August using the projected revenues and cost percentages listed above. The revenue from food, beverages, and other income was estimated based on last year's results and business booked to date.

Danielle's projected changes in some costs were based on the following predictions:

- The food cost percentage will be lowered by enforcing portion control and standardized recipe procedures.
- The Atrium restaurant and kitchen salaries will be lowered by eliminating overtime.
- The room service salaries will increase when a tray-setup helper is hired because of customer complaints about slow service.
- The F&B management salaries and payroll taxes and benefits will be based on projected salary and bonus increases.
- The increase in the napery and uniforms category will include replacement of breakfast napkins and kitchen outfits.
- Fewer china, glass, and silver utensils are scheduled to be purchased this year.
- The breakfast paper napkins will be replaced by cloth napkins.

THE PROFIT AND LOSS STATEMENT

The **profit and loss (P&L) statement** is a financial report that summarizes business transactions during an accounting period, generally for 1 month. Other names for this report are **earning statement**, **income statement**, and **operating statement**. The P&L statement in lodging establishments is compiled by department. The reports of all departments are summarized in a statement usually called the **consolidated P&L statement**. P&L statements are divided into two sections: **current month** and **year to date**. The current month column shows the results for a particular month, and the year to date the results for the accumulated time since the beginning of the fiscal year. The categories in these sections match those of the annual budget. The purpose of the departmental P&L statement is to show the results of the operational activity of each department. The purpose of the consolidated P&L statement is to analyze the present situation regarding the overall profit or loss of the property's business activity.

SITUATION 8.4   A P&L Statement for the F&B Department

During the first week of September, the results of operations at the hotel described in Situation 8.3 for the month of August had been calculated. The revenues and expenses for the F&B department were as follows:

Food Revenue

Atrium restaurant	17,204 covers @ $6.10/average check
Room service	3,981 covers @ $6.50/average check
Banquets	6,030 covers @ $7.15/average check

Beverage Revenue

Applause	10,142 covers @ $4.32/average check
Atrium restaurant	$5,643
Room service	$3,780
Banquets	$6,092

Other Income

Room rentals	$8,342
Other	$3,690

Cost of Sales

Cost of food	33.3%
Cost of beverage	23.1%

Salaries and Wages

Atrium salaries	21.5%
Room service salaries	23.5%
Banquet salaries	10.9%
Applause salaries	13.9%
Kitchen salaries	14.2%
F&B management salaries	2.1%

Payroll Taxes and Benefits	8.6%

Other Expenses

Outside services	0.7%
Cleaning supplies	0.4%
Napery	1.1%
Guest supplies	0.2%
China, glass and silver	0.5%
Music and entertainment	1.2%
Printing and stationery	0.2%
Uniforms	0.4%
Paper supplies	0.1%
Incentives	0.4%

ASSIGNMENT: You have recently been hired as the hotel's assistant controller. Prepare the profit and loss statement for the F&B department for the month of August (omitting the year-to-date section). Include the gross profit and the income in dollars and as a percentage.

VARIANCE ANALYSIS BETWEEN THE BUDGET AND THE P&L STATEMENT

A comparison between the P&L statement and the budget makes it possible for management to find out the changes that have taken place in the budgeted amounts as a result of operations. The changes can be higher or lower than the budgeted figures. If the revenue and income results are higher, the difference is favorable; if the cost results are higher, the difference is unfavorable (and vice versa).

Usually, variance analyses are compiled monthly in hospitality operations. They allow management to identify the causes of the negative results so that operational adjustments can be effected to correct any problems.

SITUATION 8.5 Variance Analysis Between Budget and P&L Statement

As assistant rooms division manager of a 310-room hotel in Denver, Colorado, you have been provided with the P&L statement for March (actual results). You also know the budgeted amounts for each rooms division category for the same period. The figures for "actual" and "budgeted" are as shown below.

Rooms Division	Actual	Percentage	Budgeted	Percentage
Revenue	$473,979	100.0	$541,800	100.0
Salaries and Wages				
Front office	22,219	4.7	24,925	4.6
Housekeeping	60,786	12.8	43,890	8.1
Payroll Taxes and Benefits	23,598	5.0	19,393	3.6
Other Expenses				
Travel commissions	10,112	2.1	11,110	2.1
Cleaning supplies	538	0.1	1,085	0.2
Linen replacement	1,055	0.2	3,795	0.7
Guest supplies	5,647	1.2	6,550	1.2
Telephone	2,063	0.4	2,650	0.5
Printing and stationery	1,546	0.3	1,625	0.3
Laundry supplies	1,008	0.2	1,630	0.3
Incentive plan	266	0.1	1,600	0.3
Auto expense	3,033	0.6	3,026	0.6
Miscellaneous expenses	882	0.2	940	0.2
Departmental Profit	341,226	72.0	419,581	77.4

ASSIGNMENT: Compile the **variance analysis** for March, indicating dollars and percentage variance for each category. Identify major discrepancies, comment on the results, and propose possible ways to reduce costs to budgeted levels.

PHYSICAL INVENTORIES

Graduates from hotel and restaurant management programs are usually involved, as soon as they join the industry, in taking and analyzing **physical inventories**—the actual counting and pricing of assets. The supplies and material used in restaurant and lodging operations are considerable. Inventories facilitate the function of controlling their costs. The purpose of taking physical inventories is to find out how many items of each category are on hand and to work out their current market value. Once the value of items used in a period of time has been ascertained, the costs are expensed against the revenue generated for the same period and the percentages obtained compared with the amounts budgeted for the different categories. The cost of items used is determined by adding the total purchases during the month to the opening inventory and subtracting the merchandise on hand as per the physical inventory for each category.

SITUATION 8.6   The Role of Physical Inventories in Controlling Costs

Tim Badilla is the assistant controller of a 390-room economy hotel in downtown St. Louis. Tim has been asked by his boss to monitor the use of laundry chemicals consumed by the establishment because the cost percentages have been climbing steadily in the last 3 months. It is late evening on Monday, May 31. Tim has found the following amounts of laundry chemicals in both the main hotel storeroom and the laundry department:

Main Storeroom

      15 cases of detergent at $90 each

      15 cases of neutralizer at $65 each

      16 cases of softener at $31 each

      7 pails of bleach at $7.50 each

      1 bucket of starch at $13.50 each

Laundry Room

      5.75 cases of detergent

      2.25 cases of neutralizer

      8.50 cases of softener

      0.50 pails of bleach

      0.25 buckets of starch

The beginning inventory for laundry supplies on May 1 was $6,051.75. Purchases of laundry chemicals on May 9 totaled $890.15. The hotel sold 9,067 rooms for the week at an average daily rate of $65.10. The average daily rate was as budgeted. The budgeted laundry chemicals cost percentage was 0.2.

ASSIGNMENT: Find the actual laundry chemical cost percentage for the month and analyze and critique the result. If the difference between actual and budgeted cost percentages is found to be substantial, offer possible reasons for the discrepancy.

INVENTORY TURNOVER

Most hospitality enterprises follow operational practices aimed at conserving cash. One of these practices is keeping food and beverage inventories as low as possible. Operators must balance the possibility of running out of products with the chance of overinvesting in inventory, tying up cash that could be earning interest in the bank. Typically, inventory turnover ranges between two and four times per month. The turnover rate for food and for beverage is calculated by dividing the **food cost** by the **average inventory**.

SITUATION 8.7   Inventory Turnover

Justin Bridges has just begun a new job as an accounting clerk in a busy restaurant in Providence, Rhode Island. As a first assignment he has been asked to figure out the food inventory turnover for June. Justin obtained the beginning of the month inventory taken on May 31; the total was $25,650. The end of the month inventory, obtained on June 30, totaled $24,002 and the purchases for the month totaled $85,514.

ASSIGNMENT: Calculate the turnover inventory of the restaurant, then indicate what would happen if the turnover were reduced to two times. Specifically, would management have more or less money to invest?

FOOD AND BEVERAGE COST CONTROL

Although the calculation of food and beverage cost percentages is very simple (dividing the total cost of sales by the revenue), ascertaining the exact amount that represents the total cost of sales is not at all easy. For example, the **total food consumed** must be credited when a jar of Spanish olives or maraschino cherries is issued to the bar; similarly, the bar (beverage) must be given credit when a bottle of Marsala wine is issued to the kitchen to prepare a chicken dish (interdepartmental credit). In addition, an exhaustive control of merchandise received and issued must take place to achieve accurate food cost percentages.

SITUATION 8.8   Food Cost Reconciliation

As controller of a resort in the Bahamas, you are about to calculate the food cost percentage for the month of July. The following information has been gathered for this task.

- Beginning inventory in main storeroom on 6/30 $19,541
- Beginning inventory in food outlets on 6/30   6,932
- Purchases to main storeroom in July   73,021
- Direct purchases to kitchen in July   12,883
- Food issued from main storeroom to food outlets   61,315

- Steward sales from main storeroom   790
- Food issued to beverage outlets   313
- Entertainment and promotion checks   2,010
- Management-signed checks   691
- Documented food spoilage   39
- Beverage issued to main kitchen   114
- Credit to food for employee meals   4,795
- Credit for happy hour hors d'oeuvres   3,040
- Physical ending inventory in main storeroom on 7/31   29,515
- Physical ending inventory in food outlets on 7/31   6,318

ASSIGNMENT: Reconcile all transactions, indicating the total food consumed, and the overage/shortage that may have taken place in the main storeroom. The total revenue for July was $191,118. Calculate the food cost percentage for this month.

KEY CONCEPTS/TERMS

average inventory
beverage revenue
consolidated P&L statement
consolidated room sales statement
cost of sales
current month
departmental budget
earning statement
estimated direct expenses
estimated revenue
fiscal year
fixed budget
food cost
food revenue

gross profit
income
income statement
interdepartmental credit
occupancy costs
operating expenses
operating statement
physical inventory
profit and loss (P&L) statement
profit before occupancy costs
short-term
total food consumed
variance analysis
year to date

Chapter 9

Hospitality Accounting

CHAPTER OBJECTIVES

- Review the format and purpose of the balance sheet.
- Describe short-term and long-term cash-flow budgets.
- Understand the concept of asset depreciation.
- Explain the relationship between cost, profit, and sales to determine the company's break-even point and the generation of a desired income.
- Calculate financial ratios.

OVERVIEW

The overall purpose of hospitality accounting is to identify and record financial issues, and to generate information about the company's assets, liabilities and investments. We look at operational accounting procedures, that focus primarily on maximizing revenues and minimizing costs, as well as managerial accounting that deals with short-term and long-term financial matters, such as cash flow management, depreciation of assets, and the relationship between cost, profit, and sales. Because financial ratios are basic to the control of operations, future hospitality managers must be able to understand and interpret them.

While chapter 8 dealt with operational concepts, including budgeting, P&L statements, variance analysis, inventories, and F&B cost control—all essential concepts for lower-level managers—chapter 9 deals with financial matters that should be of interest to hospitality graduates who hope to progress up the managerial ladder.

THE BALANCE SHEET

The **balance sheet** is the statement that shows exactly what the financial position of a business is on the last day of an accounting cycle. While the profit and loss (P&L) statement shows *how* business did take place, the balance sheet shows *where* the business is. It includes the company's **assets**, **liabilities** and

capital accounts (if any). Typically, the balance sheet lists as "assets" a company's cash on hand and in banks, **accounts receivable**, inventories, **fixed assets** and any prepaid expenses. "Liabilities" usually include **accounts payable** and **long-term debt**. The difference between total assets and total liabilities represents the **owner's equity** or net worth of the business. The balance sheet equation can be expressed as

$$\text{Assets} = \text{Liabilities} + \text{Equity}$$

For comparative purposes, the balance sheet is compiled showing figures for the current period in one column and those for the same period last year in a different column. The assets to liabilities ratio should be kept at 1:1, but it is preferable for it to be higher than 2:1. The higher the ratio is, the more security the company has.

SITUATION 9.1   The Balance Sheet

Deborah Gallegos is the controller at a hotel in Fargo, North Dakota. She has gathered information to prepare the balance sheet for the establishment as of August 31. Deborah has separated the information into the following assets and liabilities:

Assets

House banks	$ 90,030
Cash in bank	11,103
Accounts receivable	235,490
Reserve for bad debts	−20,000
Inventories	136,449
Prepaid rent	5,438
Prepaid advertising	7,490
Prepaid insurance	19,413
Furniture and equipment	399,228
Operating equipment	54,632
Accumulated depreciation	−14,707

Liabilities

Accounts payable	$234,513
Advance deposits	74,096
Accrued payroll	193,665

Accrued property tax	105,090
Accrued utilities	53,112
Accrued credit card commission	25,776
Long-term debt	175,023

ASSIGNMENT: Prepare a balance sheet (without the "last-year" column) indicating the equity of the business to date.

CASH-FLOW MANAGEMENT

Hospitality operators must anticipate the availability of **cash flow** so that debts can be settled when due. This is not always easy because the flow of money into the company frequently fluctuates. For example, a resort in Arizona that is very busy during the winter months will have to make a considerable number of payments in the summer when the bills are due but when business is at its lowest level and the surplus of revenue over expenditures is minimal.

Short-term cash-flow budgets are prepared monthly, 3 months or 1 year in advance. To compile a short-range cash-flow budget, hospitality accountants must estimate the cash receipts from cash sales and from account receivable collections, as well as the cash disbursements predicted for the same period. Disbursements include purchases paid in cash, payments of account payables due, payroll checks, utilities, rent, and cash payments for supplies and other expenses. Depreciation is not considered in cash-flow projections because it is always counted as an accounting write-down of the value of assets.

SITUATION 9.2   Monthly Cash-Flow Prediction

As accountant for a Chili's restaurant in Rochester, New York, Grace Leiterman must prepare the cash-flow budget for September. Grace uses the following budgeted income and expenses for the month:

Food revenue	$105,000
Beverage revenue	$26,250
Food cost	28% of food sales
Beverage cost	22% of beverage sales
Payroll and related (100% cash)	28% of total sales
Supplies and other expenses (100% cash)	$7,875
Utilities (100% cash)	$3,937
Rent (100% cash)	$3,500
Accounts payable due in September	$49,200

The predicted cash sales percentages are 62 for food and 83 for beverage. The accounts receivable collections are estimated at 38 percent of the $44,363 credit sales in August. Eighteen percent of the current month's cost of food and 90 percent of the cost of beverage will be paid in cash, and 80 percent of accounts payable for August's $61,500 F&B purchases will be due in September.

ASSIGNMENT: Prepare a cash-flow budget for this Chili's restaurant for September. The opening cash balance on September 1 was $22,501.

Long-range cash-flow projections can be made years in advance. In this case, changes within working capital are ignored, assuming that the current asset and liability figures remain more or less constant. Long-term cash-flow budgets take into consideration the expected annual net income amount and the projected depreciation; this will constitute the company's cash position and the long-term loan payments are deducted from this amount. The purpose of long-term cash-flow projections is to foresee the availability of cash to meet long-range loan commitments.

Although graduates in entry-level positions will not be involved in long-term cash-flow projections, they should have a basic understanding of why cash availability is important to fulfill mortgage obligations and to plan for replacement or additions of capital assets.

SITUATION 9.3   Long-term Cash-Flow Projections

After his graduation from a hotel and restaurant management program, Ted Roemer decided to open and manage a restaurant. He borrowed money from his parents to buy an existing store in downtown San Antonio and secured a long-term mortgage from the bank to make much-needed pre-opening renovations of the premises. The business went well the first year of operation, and Ted decided to renovate the kitchen by changing its design to improve the traffic flow to and from the restaurant area. This time, however, Ted does not intend to borrow any additional money. Instead, he prefers to wait and use any accumulated cash flow sufficient to pay for the renovation. Ted has been given an estimate of $205,000 to finish the project. The restaurant's long-term projections were as follows:

Next Year

Net income after taxes	$28,000
Calculated depreciation	75,500
Loan payments to bank	45,000

Year 2

Net income after taxes	$37,000
Calculated depreciation	73,700
Loan payment to bank	45,000

Year 3

Net income after taxes	$44,000
Calculated depreciation	58,900
Loan payments to bank	45,000

Year 4

Net income after taxes	$49,000
Calculated depreciation	36,100
Loan payment to bank	45,000

Year 5

Net income after taxes	$52,000
Calculated depreciation	29,700
Loan payment to bank	45,000

ASSIGNMENT: Calculate the accumulated annual cash flow for the next 5 years and determine when there will be enough funds for Ted to pay in full the kitchen renovation.

DEPRECIATION

The cost of assets can be written off over their useful **life span**. Because depreciation reduces net income in an accounting period, income tax is also reduced, increasing cash flow for the same accounting cycle. This depreciation, which is regulated by the Internal Revenue Service (IRS), is considered as an expense of the business, as are salaries, utilities, and other expenses. In hospitality accounting, 7 years are usually assigned for fixed assets (FF&E) and over 30 years for buildings. Land, as an asset, is not depreciated because it is considered to have an indefinite life span. There are two common methods of calculating depreciation: **straight-line depreciation** and **declining-balance depreciation**.

Straight-line Depreciation

Companies that use straight-line depreciation calculate the depreciation of an asset by spreading its cost over each year of its life span. Thus, a $21,000 asset with a life span of 7 years can be depreciated by $3,000 annually (21,000 : 7 = 3,000).

Declining-balance Depreciation

This method allows for a 200 percent write-off on a declining basis. That is, for an asset with a life span of 7 years the depreciation rate will be 28.58 percent annually ($100 : 7 = 14.29$; $14.29 \times 2 = 28.58$). Using this method, the first year write-off will be 28.58 percent of the cost; the second year write-off will be 28.58 percent of the cost minus the first year's depreciation; and so on.

SITUATION 9.4   Asset Depreciation

Sam Lee has been hired by a restaurant chain as the regional accountant for three units in the Midwest. One of his priorities was to increase the company's cash flow for the next three years. On inspecting the current accounting procedures, Sam discovers that his predecessor used the straight-line method to depreciate fixed assets. He wondered if by changing this procedure to the declining-balance method of depreciation the shortage of cash could be alleviated. To find out, he considered the impending purchase of furniture for a new restaurant being opened. The initial cost of the furniture was $118,000 and the depreciation period was 7 years.

ASSIGNMENT: Calculate the annual depreciation for the new furniture over the 7-year life span using the straight-line and the declining-balance methods and decide which one would increase the cash flow of the company over the next 3 years.

THE COST-PROFIT-SALES RELATIONSHIP

After working out variable and fixed costs for a business cycle, hospitality operators often want to find out the level of sales that need to be generated to cover these costs or to generate a predetermined income. These answers can be obtained by dividing the fixed costs plus the profit sought by 100 percent minus the variable costs as a percentage of the revenue. However, these calculations are in practice only approximate because there are several factors that can distort the results once operations take place. But these figures do provide operators with a general idea of the volume necessary to achieve certain operational objectives.

SITUATION 9.5   Understanding the Cost-Profit-Sales Relationship

Ann Pistolesi has been promoted to manager of a soon-to-be-opened 400-room La Quinta-franchised hotel in Portland, Oregon. Working closely with the controller, Ann started to put together the first annual budget by asking all line managers to staff their departments for salaried and hourly positions. The projected occupancy percentage for the first year was set at 52. To be competitive with other hotels in the area, the rooms division director and the sales and marketing manager recommended an ADR of $69 for the first year. All managers were then asked to provide monthly operational costs for their departments. Ann received the following the information, consolidated for the year:

Departmental expenses (variable cost)		$1,246,628
Deductions from operations (variable cost)		
Administrative and general	$822,326	
Franchise fee	57,445	
Sales and promotion	422,876	
Management fee	335,373	
Property operation	406,900	
Energy costs	296,551	
Deductions from operations total		2,341,471
Capital expenses (fixed cost)		
Rent-lease	780,568	
Mortgage	393,510	
Capital expenses total		1,174,078

ASSIGNMENT: At this point, Ann wants to know if the volume of sales predicted would be sufficient to (1) break even and (2) generate an income of $650,000.

FINANCIAL RATIOS

Two of the most critical challenges hospitality managers-in-training face as they start their careers are the calculation *and* interpretation of financial ratios. The ratios that supervisors and managers use most are calculated from operational data gathered in income statements and balance sheets. There are several important operational ratios that can be worked out from income statements:

- **Occupancy percentage.** *Rooms sold : rooms available*
  This ratio explains the management's ability to sell rooms. The U.S. rate for hotel average room occupancy has been between 60 and 70 percent.
- **Cost of labor percentage.** *Payroll + related expenses : total revenue*
  This ratio is useful to monitor labor costs. It can be interpreted as an indicator of productivity. Average percentages depend on the property and on the department. A "normal" rooms division ratio would be between 18 and 22 percent of sales. A "normal" F&B department ratio for a full-service property would be 35 to 45 percent of total F&B sales.
- **Cost of food sold percentage.** *Cost of food sold : food sales*
  This ratio shows the profitability of food sales. A higher ratio than

budgeted usually indicates the need for better control. Average percentages depend on the type of operation. Although a quick-service restaurant could have a percentage as low as 25, a full-service hotel may run food-cost percentages between 35 and 45.

- **Cost of beverage sold percentage.** *Cost of beverage sold : beverage sales*
As with the cost of food sold percentage, this ratio compares cost of the product to product sales. Averages for the industry depend on the type of property and the quality of the product served. An independent bar could cut the percentage to between 15 and 20 while that of a full-service property usually ranges between 20 and 25.

- **Average daily rate (ADR).** *Room revenue : paid room nights*
This dollar figure is key to generating income. If costs are kept under control, a higher rate will increase the property's bottom line.

- **Profit margin.** *Income : revenue*
This ratio indicates the property's bottom line: measuring the management's ability to generate revenue and to control expenses, it is the measure of profitability. Profit margins for the rooms division of well-managed hotels range from 70 to 75 percent. Profit margins for F&B departments should range between 15 and 25 percent on average.

- **Total revenue change from budget.** *Actual revenue − budgeted revenue : budgeted revenue*
This ratio indicates the situation relative to budgeted sales. It reflects whether an individual department or property is ahead of or behind its projected revenues.

- **Housekeeping cost for occupied room.** *Total housekeeping costs : total rooms sold*
This ratio indicates how costs are being controlled in the housekeeping department by comparing them with budgeted amounts.

- **Rooms sales to total sales.** *Rooms revenue : total revenue*
Generally, rooms are the major generators of revenue in lodging properties. A high percentage is usually a strong indicator of profitability.

- **Total rooms division payroll per occupied room.** *Total rooms division payroll : rooms sold*
This is a measure of productivity for the rooms division. The lower the number, the higher the productivity will be.

SITUATION 9.6   Financial Ratios from Income Statements

The departmental income statements given below correspond to the month of March for a 310-room hotel in Costa Mesa, California. The first statement is for the rooms division, and the second for the F&B division of the establishment. In the interest of space, the expense categories have been, in some cases, combined.

Rooms Division Report

	Actual	Budgeted
Rooms Revenue	$473,979	$541,800
Total Payroll and Related		
Front office	28,219	33,605
Housekeeping	48,833	57,283
Other Expenses		
Front office	16,754	18,411
Housekeeping	9,396	15,600
Departmental Income	370,777	416,901

F&B Report

	Actual	Budgeted
F&B Revenue		
Food	$220,728	$210,095
Beverage	70,578	78,706
Other income	10,882	12,000
Cost of Sales		
Food	85,840	68,481
Beverage	16,177	17,709
Total F&B Payroll and Related	113,439	122,692
Other Expenses	20,076	30,052
Departmental Income	66,656	61,867

ASSIGNMENT: Tom Vallen, assistant manager of the hotel, has been asked to calculate and interpret the following ratios: occupancy percentage; cost of labor percentage for rooms and F&B; cost of food sold percentage; cost of beverage sold percentage; average daily rate; profit margin for rooms and F&B; total revenue change from budget for rooms and F&B; housekeeping cost per occupied room; rooms sales to total sales; total rooms division payroll per occupied room. What will be the results? The number of rooms sold for the month was 7,755.

KEY CONCEPTS/TERMS

accounts payable
accounts receivable
assets
balance sheet
capital accounts
cash flow
declining-balance depreciation

fixed assets
liabilities
life span
long-term debt
owner's equity
straight-line depreciation

PART 2

Management Experiences in Hospitality

Chapter 10

Strategic Planning and Management

CHAPTER OBJECTIVES

- Understand the nature and purpose of strategic planning.
- Describe how to conduct a SWOT analysis.
- Learn to resolve case studies.
- Discuss the concept of strategic management.
- Learn about developing a company's vision.
- Practice setting and implementing strategic objectives.

OVERVIEW

It is easy to predict that graduates of hotel and restaurant management programs who have been hired by hospitality companies will be promptly promoted to management positions after a period of training, practice in supervisory operations, and learning about the tactical planning involved in day-to-day activities. Also, it is not uncommon for instructors to learn that one of their students who graduated only a few years back is engaged in regional management, responsible for the operations and planning of several hospitality units. For this reason, all students hoping to become managers in the hospitality industry should acquire knowledge of long-range planning and management.

It may be possible that, after some years in the industry, a hospitality program graduate is given the opportunity of becoming the chief executive officer of a large company or corporation. Such a position implies setting long-term strategic tasks that include the development of a strategic mission and setting strategic objectives as well as determining criteria for achieving these objectives. All along in this process, the chief executive officer must initiate and implement any corrective adjustments or changes leading to the success of the enterprise as a whole.

STRATEGIC PLANNING

All businesses, large or small, must compete in the market with their services and products, hospitality operations being no exception. Hospitality managers spend a great deal of time developing plans to adapt to changing conditions and compete successfully in the business environment. For this purpose, they must identify goals and how these will be achieved. Several questions should be asked during the strategic planning process:

- What changes are to be effected regarding markets, services, and operations?
- How will the new directions be coordinated and implemented?
- What resources must be allocated to reach the desired objectives?

For example, at the operational level, the manager of a restaurant who wants to start attracting college students on weekends must think about the effect the new clientele will have on the current customer mix. By attracting young, lively patrons the establishment may lose its current family business. If a preliminary analysis shows that the decision to attract college students will be beneficial to the bottom line, what changes in advertising, restaurant décor, service and overall ambience will be necessary? Will the resources invested in the changes result in overall positive gains?

Strategic planning can be performed at corporate, regional, or property levels. An example of corporate-level strategic planning would be the acquisition of capital for corporate expansion. At a regional level, planning usually focuses on the marketing of the product in a specific area of the country or state—for example, the regional office of a hotel chain in Arizona being concerned with attracting international travelers that arrive regularly to Phoenix in charter flights on their way to the Grand Canyon. A typical strategic planning example at a property level would be to expand the convention facilities of a resort located near the future site of a manufacturing company's national headquarters.

Strategic planning often involves **SWOT analysis**—a classic operational strategic planning model that can be summarized in the four words represented in its acronym: (1) strengths, (2) weaknesses, (3) opportunities, and (4) threats. This theory requires that an internal analysis of the business and an external investigation of the competitive environment are conducted prior to the decision-making period. In other words, managers must ask questions related to internal issues: What **strengths** does the company or property have? What **weaknesses** does it face? For example, if a hotel is located in the center of a city, will traffic and parking be a problem? Even if the hotel is an excellent property, it will be inadvisable to spend a lot of effort and resources to attract overnight guests passing through a highway several miles away. Managers must also ask about external issues: What **opportunities** and **threats** exist in the business environment? For instance, if an establishment is old and rundown, it will be necessary to refurbish it if a new competitive property is being opened nearby. A property's SWOT operational components might include the following typical examples:

S: Internal strengths	Well-trained, professional staff
	Easily accessible location
W: Internal weaknesses	Limited meeting space
	Obsolete operating equipment
	Lack of technological tools
O: External opportunities	Lack of nearby business competition
	Booming local economy
T: External threats	Strong business competition
	Declining local economy

After a SWOT analysis is conducted, management will be faced with the following possible scenarios:

1. *Internal strengths are substantial and external opportunities are good.* In this case, the company should capitalize on existing favorable conditions to maximize revenue. An aggressive operational strategy should be adopted.

2. *Internal strengths are substantial and external threats are major.* In this case, the company must identify and adopt a market niche to attract as much of the limited business available as possible—for example, by advertising the best customer service in town. A strategy to expand in this case would be inadvisable. '

3. *Internal weaknesses are substantial and external opportunities are good.* In this case, the strategic plan should focus on eliminating the deficiencies in order to take advantage of the positive external environment—for example, by building additional meeting space to accommodate existing demand. The strategy should focus on the turnaround of the property.

4. *Internal weaknesses are substantial and external threats are major.* In this case, it may not be a good idea to build additional meeting space if customer demand does not exist. The strategy should be to address current weaknesses but without investing considerable additional resources.

In all cases and at all levels (corporate, regional, and property), when planning strategically, there must be a clear identification of purpose toward which all planning efforts must be directed. Specific questions should thus be asked:

What should the product offered be?

What level of quality is to be achieved?

What value/price ratio is expected to be perceived by guests?

Let's look at two case studies similar to those that may be encountered by hospitality graduates.

CASE 10.1 Strategic Planning for the Oxford Hotel

The Oxford Hotel was inaugurated in Lincoln, Nebraska, in 1944. For years, the establishment was the indisputable headquarters for visitors from the surrounding area and the center of activity for the community, patronized by the most prominent local families and business leaders. The Oxford, which in the past offered fine dining and banquet services unmatched by the competition, was listed on the National Register of Historic Places. For the last 5 years, however, the return on investment to owners had been less than desirable. The reason, according to the hotel's management, was competition created by two newly opened chain-operated establishments located within walking distance of the Oxford. The new hotels benefited from strong nationwide advertising and marketing campaigns and from belonging to a central reservation system network.

Many of the formerly staunch community supporters of the Oxford were torn between patronizing the nostalgic, historic landmark and enjoying the modern amenities offered by the new properties. The owners, of necessity, decided to hire a consultant to find out what could be done to return the Oxford to acceptable profitability levels. The first step proposed by the consultant consisted of conducting a shop audit, followed by an interview with the current general manager. The following is a copy of the report sent to the owners by the consultant:

> I started the shop audit by telephoning the hotel directly to reserve a room at 11 AM on Monday. The operator answered the call after five rings and connected me with reservations. The clerk, very courteously, took down the information and confirmed that she was giving me a "special rate for a standard room." I had not asked for a special rate; in fact, I would have preferred a junior suite or similar accommodation as I was traveling with my 10-year-old son.
>
> When we arrived at the hotel by cab, there was no doorman at the entrance of the hotel. We carried our luggage into the lobby where a bellperson offered to take our suitcases. The lobby was impressive, with dark oak paneling and furniture. The elevator doors were finished in laminated burnished copper. The décor conveyed a formal elegance. There were two clerks at the front desk: one was busy entering data into a computer terminal and the other was speaking to a guest at the counter. It might have been 4 minutes before the person at the computer greeted me and offered help.
>
> The hallway leading to our room was so dark that the room numbers were difficult to read. I counted three breakfast trays and one ice bucket with an empty wine bottle outside the rooms. It was 4 PM. The first impression of the room was that of being old and decayed. The carpet had a few dark spots and the wallpaper behind the night table was starting to peel off. A lightbulb in one of the standing lamps was burned out. The bathroom was well lit. The mirror had a brown mark at its bottom edge, a sign that humidity had deteriorated the backing. The caulking around the tub was dark and chipped near the drain valve.

After washing up, we went down to the restaurant to have dinner. The décor of the room was overwhelming, with thick, red curtains covering the windows, a dark-crimson carpet, and ornate gold molding festooning the ceiling. The menu was difficult to read because of the lack of adequate light. The food was delicious, but we had to wait 1 hour and 15 minutes for the waiter to serve it.

After paying the bill, we went to the bar for a drink. I ordered a whiskey and soda and a ginger ale for my son. The waitress did not ask me what type of whiskey I wanted nor did she try to upsell the order to a premium drink. When I asked for the bill, she told me the amount without presenting a check.

After returning to our room, we found that the beds were comfortable but the air-conditioning system was noisy, clanking loudly during the night every time it turned on and off. The next morning, after discovering that the shower had strong hot and cold surges, we decided to take a bath rather than risk being scalded. We ordered room service and were served an elegant breakfast. The cart was neatly arranged with silver-plated utensils and a fresh flower in a crystal vase. Breakfast was hot and appetizing but it took 55 minutes for it to be brought to the room from the time we ordered it.

At checkout, there was a line of guests with only one clerk visible. After several minutes, the clerk opened a side door and asked for help. The front desk supervisor came out and the line split in two. My bill had a phone charge that was not mine. The clerk disappeared into the back office and reappeared with a bundle of vouchers that backed up the charge on the folio. After some discussion, the clerk agreed that the amount had been posted to my account by mistake.

Interview with the Property's General Manager

According to the general manager, the cost of energy is very high, and the hotel does not have an energy control system. There is also a lack of storage space that makes the control of inventories difficult; most of the food purchases go directly to the kitchen when they are delivered. There is no concierge floor for frequent or special guests. The Oxford has no game room for young travelers and no special amenities for children. There is no health club, exercise room, or swimming pool. The hotel does not belong to a national reservation system. Banquet services are very good and the hotel can accommodate functions up to 1,000 guests; the number of breakout rooms, however, is insufficient for large conventions.

Operational Statistics

Occupancy:	Last year's occupancy was 59%.
	Average occupancy for the area is 73%.
	Hotel's occupancy percentage dropped 20% in last five years.
Average Daily Rate:	Current ADR is $158.
	Hotel has maintained its ADR level for last 5 years.
Percentage of room revenue to total revenue:	62 last year
	80 five years ago

Profit for the last 5 years:	Year 5	$285,414
	Year 4	193,070
	Year 3	84,552
	Year 2	83,913
	Last year	−35,015

Personnel   To adjust for diminishing returns, management at the Oxford has been steadily reducing the number of employees. In years past, the ratio of employee per guest was 1:1; now it is 1:3. The following salaried positions have been eliminated in the last 5 years:

- 2 sales representatives
- 2 front desk supervisors
- 2 engineering specialists
- 1 manager on duty (weekends)
- 1 sous-chef
- 2 dining room shift supervisors

Guest Comments   Most complaints on guest comment cards were related to services and facilities:

- The service is not as good as it once was.
- The hotel is not as clean as it used to be.
- There is no health club, exercise room, or swimming pool at the Oxford.

ASSIGNMENT:

- Conduct a SWOT analysis of the Oxford.
- Identify strategic problems.
- Evaluate possible operational, marketing, and financial strategic alternatives.
- Determine the new value/price to be perceived by guests.
- Propose a timetable for a plan of action.

What specific changes are to be recommended regarding the marketing, services, and operations of the hotel?

STRATEGIC MANAGEMENT

The main goal of strategic management is to develop a company's **strategic vision**—the roadmap for short- and long-term directions achieved by setting performance objectives. In the course of the implementation phase, management must be ready to change the patterns of activity as situations require.

Strategic Vision Development

Companies, particularly large companies, usually have their business missions—what they produce and how they sell the product—clearly defined. Strategic vision goes beyond that, defining the essence of an enterprise in the long term. It is the course that a company must follow for an indefinite period. It provides the answers to key questions: Where and how do we want to expand? Is there a need for regrouping? What new technology should our business units adopt? How will our customers perceive our company? A strategic vision can be expressed in a single statement; such as "Our mission is to be one of America's best restaurant chains by (1) providing our customers with an authentic, superior-quality product, (2) offering unparalleled customer service, and (3) being committed to community service wherever we operate."

Setting Strategic Objectives

Strategic objectives are a series of performance targets, results, and outcomes that an organization seeks to accomplish. Derived from the strategic vision statement, they serve as standards of measurement for a company's strategic performance. Some companies decide to set business objectives that are reasonably achievable, whereas others focus on more aggressive, challenging roles. Whenever possible, objectives should be quantitatively stated in order to facilitate their measurement. For example, it is easier to measure a business objective stated as "$3 million in sales" than one stated as "a large volume of sales." Another example of a tangible strategic objective is "to be ranked fourth nationally by the volume of sales achieved."

When objectives are set for monetary receipts or expenditures, they are referred to as **financial objectives**. An example might be "to achieve an annual growth in earnings per share of 8 percent or higher."

Implementing the Strategy

After determining the strategic objectives, the next logical step is to implement them. This strategic phase involves a series of tasks related to the managerial functions that are necessary components of the strategic objective implementation process. Such tasks might include the following:

- Allocation of resources
- Establishment of operating procedures
- Creation of a company/corporate culture
- Building an appropriate working environment
- Motivation of employees
- Creation of an efficient communication framework
- Establishment of a community relations program

CASE 10.2   Strategic Management for Peter Pan Pizza

Brandon Robbins has been working in the hospitality industry for several years. His career has included operational positions with three major nationwide chains. His last job with Pizza Shack Inc. consisted of managing two local stores in the Montgomery, Alabama, area. A talented, hardworking individual, Brandon was not afraid of spending 15 hours on the job, 7 days a week. Looking for advancement in his career, he accepted the position of manager of Peter Pan Pizza, a small company founded in Mobile three years ago by two local entrepreneurs.

Brandon spent some time in his new job analyzing the company's financial position and its human resources and marketing issues. After completing the analysis, he was not sure that leaving his successful job in Montgomery to become manager for Peter Pan had been a good idea. Nevertheless, it was now too late, and he decided to do his best to bring his new company out of a difficult situation and into a solvent, successful enterprise. The report, typed by Brandon's secretary from his numerous notes and comments, follows.

Company Structure

The Peter Pan Pizza headquarters is located in Mobile, Alabama. The company consists of four stores located around the city. Store 1, the first unit opened by the company in the early 1990s, is located in the downtown financial district. Its reputation is very good and business is quite active during lunchtime on weekdays, serving patrons from the numerous business offices nearby. Evening business is usually slow because few people reside in the downtown area. Many customers, most of them female, have been complaining for quite some time about the lack of "fresh" items on the menu. The only fresh item, they say, is garden salad with a choice of two dressings: Italian and blue cheese. A rumor has been circulating that a nearby hamburger restaurant is being converted into a franchised Capone's pizza restaurant.

Store 2 is in a busy shopping center near the university. Business in this store is fair during the evening and on weekends with many delivery orders. This store was very successful until Mama Joan's Pizza started operations on the next block; since then, business has slowed down considerably. Store 3 is located on a busy street, a business loop of Interstate 10. Parking is good and the entrance to the store is on the right side of the main traffic pattern. Business is brisk from opening to closing. There is no pizza competitor in the area. Store 4 is situated in Mobile's main shopping mall. Business is excellent on weekends and when the mall has special promotion days. There is a Cineplex movie theater nearby that generates sales late in the evening.

The company's president is Tony Bianchi, an 11-year veteran of the industry. Frequently, he likes to travel to the four locations and help with hands-on work if necessary. Tony is very knowledgeable about operations but lacks financial and marketing know-how. When Brandon was hired, Tony asked him to make all necessary decisions—operational, financial, and marketing-related—to turn around the situation of the four stores. As he put it, "I want you to take care of the strategic management of the company." Tony is aware that the company as a whole is not doing very well. He thinks the organization would be rejuvenated by opening a couple of stores in Huntsville, where there is no major competition, and perhaps one in Birmingham.

Store Operations

The four stores are open 7 days a week, from 11 AM to 1 AM. The busiest periods vary by store. The downtown unit is very busy Monday through Thursday at lunchtime. All stores are extremely busy on weekends from 4 PM to 8 PM. Six drivers are generally needed on Friday nights, but one is usually sufficient during slow periods. The company's policy is to deliver pizza within a 30-minute time limit.

Bakers and order-takers are paid between $7 and $9 per hour. Drivers receive minimum wage plus mileage. Each store operates with a manager that is in charge of keeping track of inventory, hiring, training, and controlling the store's receipts.

Staffing

As with most quick-service operations, Peter Pan Pizza has always maintained that the key to success depends on hiring and training its employees well. Creating a work environment conducive to teamwork is critical to achieving high productivity.

Because of high employee turnover, store managers have to work long hours most of the time as well as deal with constant staffing problems due to absenteeism. But store managers can earn a substantial income, which may be as high as $50,000 per year. Salaries average $31,000 but include a bonus of 12 percent of the store's profit. Individual store business always suffers when a well-trained, reliable store manager quits. Only one of the four store managers has stayed with the company more than 5 years. Attracting and keeping part-time employees is also a problem. This is caused mainly by the split-shifting required to fit the schedule and the inability of the company to guarantee a minimum of hours per week in most cases.

On average, the payroll per store includes the manager and 20 part-time bakers, order-takers, and drivers. However, because of turnover and absenteeism, the stores are chronically understaffed and service suffers seriously.

Store Profitability

A summary of this year's operations to date for each store is shown in Exhibit 1. The year-to-date figures represent the totals for 9 months of business, from the start of the fiscal year on July 1 through March 31 of the following year.

Exhibit 1   Summary of Operations by Store

	Store 1	
	Current Month	**Year to Date**
Revenue		
Net sales	$32,550	$309,551
Cost of sales	7,486	65,374
Gross Profit	25,064	244,177
Variable Expenses		
Total labor cost	14,647	138,092
Other expenses	4,882	34,938
Fixed	5,859	52,731
Total expenses	25,388	225,761
Income (Loss)	$ 324	$ 18,416

	Store 2	
	Current Month	**Year to Date**
Revenue		
Net sales	$24,800	$235,200
Cost of sales	6,200	59,800
Gross Profit	18,600	175,400
Variable Expenses		
Total labor cost	7,688	67,192
Other expenses	4,503	40,604
Fixed	7,040	63,360
Total expenses	19,231	171,156
Income (Loss)	$ (631)	$ (4,244)

	Store 3	
	Current Month	**Year to Date**
Revenue		
Net sales	$37,975	$335,775
Cost of sales	8,354	73,871
Gross Profit	29,621	261,904
Variable Expenses		
Total labor cost	10,253	90,659
Other expenses	2,658	30,220
Fixed	4,091	36,040
Total expenses	17,002	156,919
Income (Loss)	$12,619	$104,985

	Store 4	
	Current Month	**Year to Date**
Revenue		
Net sales	$34,534	$313,002
Cost of sales	8,979	71,485
Gross Profit	25,555	241,517
Variable Expenses		
Total labor cost	8,979	84,511
Other expenses	3,798	28,170
Fixed	5,300	47,700
Total expenses	18,077	160,381
Income (Loss)	$ 7,478	$ 81,136

Financial Position

Exhibit 2 is a summary consolidated statement of operations for last year. It provides the operating revenue and expenses, the change in net assets from operations, and the net assets at the end of the year.

Exhibit 2   Summary Consolidated Statement of Operations (Last Year)

Operating revenue	$1,564,490
Operating expenses	1,295,386
Change in Net Assets from Operations	269,104
Net assets (deficit) at beginning of year	305,993
Net assets at end of year	**$ 575,097**

Exhibit 3   Summary Consolidated Statement of Financial Position (Last Year)

Current assets	$ 230,094
Property and equipment	894,740
Total Assets	1,124,834
Current liabilities	105,870
Bank indebtedness	343,867
Long-term debt	100,000
Total Liabilities	549,737
Net assets	575,097
Total liabilities and net assets	**$1,124,834**

ASSIGNMENT: Put yourself in Brandon's position and answer the following strategic management questions:

- Should the company continue operations as usual?
- Should management consider selling any of the stores?
- Should they plan to start operations in other locations?
- Is the company in a healthy financial position?

After answering these questions, prepare an analysis of operations and present a strategic vision report to be proposed to Tony Bianchi along with strategic objectives.

KEY CONCEPTS/TERMS

financial objectives	strengths
opportunities	SWOT analysis
strategic objectives	threats
strategic vision	weaknesses

Chapter 11

Ethics and Hospitality Management

CHAPTER OBJECTIVES

- Review the need for a company code of ethics in hospitality operations.
- Understand the ethical implications related to seven aspects of hospitality management:

  Benchmarking
  Leadership
  Accountability
  Commitment to excellence
  Integrity
  Honesty
  Fairness

OVERVIEW

The integration of ethics in the hospitality curriculum has increased in importance as all parts of the corporate world have experienced the negative impact of the corporate accounting scandals and CEO misdeeds that have soured American consumers and investors. To be profitable, every corporation hopes to have a good reputation and the trust of the public. Although high ethical standards do not necessarily translate directly into a high profit margin, a perception of their lack can negatively affect profits—resulting in consumer and employee dissatisfaction at best and lawsuits and jail time at worst. Thus, most organizations understand the need for developing a code of ethics.

Ethics is concerned with the principles of morality, with understanding what is good and bad, with knowing what is right and wrong. Ethical standards influence actions whose consequences have an impact on human welfare (many philosophies would include here the welfare of all living things). In general, most students would agree that they would rather have a positive than a negative impact on the well-being of those around them: "What goes around comes around."

Because codes of ethics usually emphasize that ethical standards should be the highest priority, taking precedence over "other standards," companies are often faced with what is called an ethical dilemma. "Other company standards" may include maintaining a high profit margin, remaining loyal to the company, or simply earning as high a wage as possible. Hospitality students, like all students, should be presented with some criteria to make moral decisions and to understand what is perceived as ethical by the business community and the general public.

DEVELOPING A COMPANY CODE OF ETHICS

Some companies follow unwritten traditions of integrity, relying on informal approaches that are taken for granted. Employees of these companies know that honesty and accountability regarding the product or service offered to customers are matters of fact in the company's business transactions. Other organizations set up a **code of ethics** that spell out ethical requirements to be followed. Here are some ethical concerns that may confront employees:

- Adherence to the law
- Quality and safety of products
- Employee safety in the workplace
- Avoidance of conflict of interest
- Fairness in selling prices
- Honesty in financial reporting

Besides the conviction that companies must comply with ethical standards of conduct because "it is the right thing to do," most organizations are aware that ethical business practices are a vital strategic key to survival and profitability in a highly competitive environment. Wrongful actions—for example, manipulating balance sheets, not disclosing to customers that a product contains potentially harmful ingredients, raising prices exorbitantly in favorable market conditions, and exploiting workers—do not pass the test of moral scrutiny.

An effective way of incorporating ethics in the workplace is by implementing adequate training on ethical conduct, especially in areas of procurement and sales. Because the ethical beliefs of managers are usually incorporated in the company's strategy, the wrongdoing of an unethical manager can cause the entire company to be viewed as condoning wrong practices. Business practices, however, may be perceived differently from country to country. Graduates hired to work in foreign enterprises must be aware that adhering to a code of ethics may be particularly difficult when conducting business in some locations overseas, where bribery and corruption may be common practice and public officials and suppliers are accustomed to kickbacks.

BENCHMARKING AND ETHICAL CONDUCT

Benchmarking is the practice that allows a company to determine whether its business performance compares favorably with the competition. Because it entails doing cross-company comparisons and inquiring about internal procedures, benchmarking must be conducted within ethical frameworks of business behavior. In some cases, benchmarking can lead to organizations colluding to implement unfair trading practices. **Business collusion**—a secret business agreement with a competitor to fix prices—undermines free market competition and is against the law.

CASE 11.1   Business Collusion

There are two major hotels in downtown Pleasantville, the Regency and the Baymont. Both hotels are independently owned by local business leaders who, although competitors, have been friends for years. The Regency is relatively old, offering guest rooms that are comfortable but of simple décor. The food and beverage service, however, is outstanding, with courteous, dedicated employees in the fine-dining restaurant and banquet department. The Baymont is a newer property, with bright, elegantly outfitted guest rooms. The establishment, however, is perceived as being poorly cleaned and maintained. The quality of food and the service in its food outlets are not considered to be excellent by guests, who complain regularly about poor attention to detail on the part of the wait staff and of longer-than-usual waiting times in the restaurant and bar. Both properties operate at a substantial profit—the Regency capitalizing on its cuisine and service, the Baymont on its well appointed guest rooms.

Hoping to improve business still more, the owners of the two hotels decided to meet and exchange information about each other's methods of operation. It should be easy to encourage the managers of the two properties to benefit from each other's expertise; after all, the visitors to Pleasantville would find their stay enjoyable regardless of which property they chose. After trading operational data and procedures for some months, it seemed to everyone that both establishments were improving in quality. As a final gesture of cooperation, the two companies decided to unify their room reservation departments to centralize all inquiries into a single system.

It was agreed that each property would set its own room rates, except during the two weeks in April when the Pleasantville fair and rodeo celebrations took place. Because both hotels were always booked solid at that time, the room rates would be set at $110 per room per night at both properties. The regular rates, outside of the fair weeks, were set at $73 at the Regency and $85 at the Baymont.

ASSIGNMENT: Discuss this case and decide whether the well-intentioned benchmarking effort of the two hotel owners led to a situation of business collusion.

LEADERSHIP ETHICS

For hospitality organizations to be perceived as ethical, managers must exercise leadership by setting their own examples of conduct and by enforcing ethical principles at all company levels. This is not always the case. Because managers are expected to achieve preestablished financial and operational goals having to do with desirable volumes of sales or income percentages, they sometimes resort to questionable practices in order to reach these goals. Often, the reasons to engage in unfair practices may be monetary incentives tied to performance. For example, to obtain a bonus tied to operational results, a manager may decide to authorize the chef to substitute a 7 ounce instead of an 8 ounce lobster tail, expecting that the difference in weight will not be noticed by a banquet host; or he may make the decision to fire two loyal, reliable, hard-working full-time employees and hire four part-time workers to reach higher-than-budgeted labor percentages by eliminating payroll benefits.

CASE 11.2 Company Profit Versus Welfare of Employees

Bob Kempinsky is general manager of a family restaurant in a small town in the Midwest. The establishment has an excellent reputation and no direct competition. As a result, business is good and the average earnings before taxes for the last 10 years have been above the industry average. Bob is considered an excellent manager by the owners and receives substantial bonuses for achieving, and sometimes bettering, the budgeted bottom line. Bob considers himself very lucky to be operating in an area of abundant worker supply because of the absence of other restaurants in the area. The property has been able to maintain very low expenses in the categories of salaries and employee benefits.

The hourly workers in the restaurant, however, do not consider themselves so fortunate. Those in need of medical care cannot easily cover their health expenses with the wages paid by the restaurant. Last week, a group of employees representing all hourly workers asked to meet with Bob to request that the company offer medical insurance benefits as part of the compensation package. After making the necessary calculations, the manager determined that the restaurant's profit before income taxes would diminish from 27 percent of the total revenue to 23 percent. This reduction would prevent Bob's receipt of his 12 percent bonus from the net-income target that had been established at 25 percent of profit.

Bob decides to reject the petition after determining that the supply of local workers would guarantee a sufficient number of applicants willing to work for the compensation the restaurant currently offers. Bob's thinking is that as a manager, his job is to maximize profit while complying with existing labor laws.

ASSIGNMENT: Discuss this case, and decide whether Bob Kempinsky behaved ethically. Consider the potential impact that his decision will have on the stakeholders involved and on the restaurant's operations.

ETHICAL ACCOUNTABILITY

Hospitality professionals are expected to be accountable or responsible for their actions regarding the livelihood of the staff working under their management. A company's selection of a candidate for a position of responsibility is often based on whether or not that person will be able to treat others fairly. Hospitality managers are accountable for the welfare of employees they supervise because in most cases, the workers' livelihoods depend on them.

CASE 11.3 Ethics and Manager Unaccountability

Elliott Waisley was the executive chef of a large resort on an island off the Florida coast. Last year the profit of the food and beverage department had been exceedingly low due, according to management, to the high expenses of the kitchen department. The time to prepare the next year's budget had come and Elliott was asked to cut down the kitchen's costs by 5 percentage points from last year's figures. As an experienced chef, he looked closely at how he would be able to reduce expenses. He came to the conclusion that the procedures for purchasing, storing, and issuing food were well controlled, with no possibility of theft or pilfering. Elliott personally oversaw the production of food and knew that portion control, yields, and selling prices were all in line. There was no option for improvement.

Chef Waisley determined that the only category with higher than average amounts was kitchen payroll. He knew that the department was overstaffed by two sous-chefs; in fact, he had decided long ago to hire them so that it was possible for him to enjoy two consecutive days (usually weekends) without the possibility of being called to work in an emergency.

Determined to comply with the management's demand, Elliott figured out that the only possible way to reduce payroll costs was to eliminate five full-time jobs and create instead nine part-time positions paying no benefits. He calculated that the savings in this swap would easily make the 5 percentage points he was asked to reduce.

When notified of the chef's decision, the five full-time employees were extremely upset. Some of them had been working in the resort for years. They approached the F&B director complaining bitterly about the decision that they considered unfair, arguing that their livelihoods were being unjustifiably jeopardized. The division director met with Elliott about the situation and was convinced by the chef that this was the only solution to reduce costs in the kitchen department. The chef's proposal was accepted.

ASSIGNMENT: Discuss the case and determine whether Chef Waisley acted ethically in his decision to let the five full-time employees go and hire nine part-time workers in their place, in order to reduce costs (instead of eliminating one sous-chef position). Also, discuss the possible effects of his decision on the kitchen employees and on operations.

ETHICS AND THE COMMITMENT TO EXCELLENCE

Most mission statements of major hospitality companies specify that management is committed to deliver the best service possible for the price paid by guests. For example, Hilton Hotels offer guests and customers the finest accommodations, services, amenities, and value. Hospitality managers who deviate from this commitment would cheat customers in their expectations of getting their money's worth for the product or services received.

CASE 11.4   Breaking the Quality Pledge

Brittani Fletcher, catering manager of a five-star hotel in the Phoenix area, has been contacted by a tour operator representative to provide a takeaway lunch for a group of Grand Canyon-bound European tourists. The travel company has requested that the box lunch be the best quality, regardless of price. After conferring with the executive chef, Brittani proposes four gourmet luncheons at $21.50 per person. The menu chosen by the tour operator includes fruit cocktail (mango, guava, pineapple, cantaloupe, and kiwi); diced fresh Atlantic salmon with Venetian sauce; and a roast-beef sandwich.

While preparing the catered lunch, the chef notified Brittani that the shipment of fresh Atlantic salmon had been delayed by one day. The chef recommended using frozen farm-raised salmon that he buys for employee meals which would taste quite good nonetheless. Because the change of fish would lower the cost of food by $2.25 per order, the chef recommended reducing the cost per person from $21.50 to $19.25. Brittani told the chef to go ahead with the change and decided not to notify the tour operator, sure that the customers would not notice the quality difference. Moreover, the hotel would make a better food cost percentage.

ASSIGNMENT: Discuss this case and decide whether Brittani Fletcher acted ethically. How might her decision impact future business customers if the substitution were to be discovered? What would you have done in this case?

ETHICAL INTEGRITY

In order for hospitality managers to be trusted by customers and by the community in which they operate, they must demonstrate sound moral principles and character. At times, they may be faced with conflicting decisions between what is morally right and making a reasonable operational profit—an **ethical dilemma**. An example would be a manager having to decide whether to use a harmful compound that pollutes the environment or pay higher prices for a product that is biodegradable.

CASE 11.5   Ethics and the Environment

Caty Tsu is the general manager of a successful resort in North Carolina. As operator, she has managed to control costs and maintain a healthy bottom line for the last 5 years. Her continued excellent performance has resulted in substantial annual bonuses.

Last month, Caty had a meeting with a group of concerned local citizens about the fertilizer that the resort was using on the 18-hole golf course located near the city water supply reservoir. According to the group, the fertilizer used contained a strong component that could contaminate the reservoir if the chemicals reached the underground water table. They suggested that the resort used a biodegradable fertilizer containing no noxious chemicals.

After consultation with the company's lawyer, Caty finds out that there are no federal or state regulations compelling golf courses to use biodegradable fertilizers. Contamination test results for the potable water supply were negative. Nevertheless, Caty wants to comply with the concerned-citizens' request, and she asks the resort's purchasing agent to inquire about buying an environmentally friendly product. She is notified that the product would cost twice as much as the nonbiodegradable fertilizer.

Fearing that her annual bonus would be substantially smaller by increasing the cost of next year's engineering budget and reducing the overall income of the resort, Caty decides to keep using the current fertilizer.

ASSIGNMENT: Discuss this case and determine if the resort manager behaved ethically in this situation. How might her decision impact her company's reputation?

HONESTY

Being willing and able to state the truth (no matter how painful) is ethically essential. Hospitality students ready to join the workforce must be made aware that misleading or deceiving others may result in costly lawsuits and, in some cases, jail sentences.

CASE 11.6   A Fraudulent Resume

Greg Ferguson is a nontraditional student who went back to college after working several years in the hospitality industry. Greg is graduating with a bachelor's degree in hotel and restaurant management this semester. Greg's senior seminar instructor has recommended that students prepare a resume before beginning the interviewing process with companies recruiting on campus.

By the end of the semester, Greg has had an interview with a restaurant company based in Georgia. He told the recruiter that he had considerable experience working in restaurants when in fact he had worked only at the front desk and the sales department of hotels. A few days later, he received a telephone call from the company's headquarters asking him to fly to Atlanta for a second interview for the assistant restaurant manager position. Greg was also asked to bring with him an updated resume listing all his industry-related experience.

Determined to get the position, Greg decides to list on his resume 3 years of work in his hometown as assistant manager of a successful restaurant that burned to the ground some years ago. All personnel records had disappeared in the fire and Greg knew that it would be impossible for the restaurant company to verify his employment record. As a mature individual, Greg is confident that he can easily handle the requirements of the job as assistant manager. He saw the company's request for previous experience as a job requisite to be a mere formality.

ASSIGNMENT: Discuss this case and determine whether Greg Ferguson acted ethically in his dealing with the recruiting company. What might result from his decision to deceive his potential employer?

FAIRNESS

A basic ethical tenet is to deal fairly with people regarding equal performance. In violation of this principle, some managers exhibit discrimination regarding sex, race, and age as well as dealing with **undocumented aliens**—illegal residents who work in the United States, usually without a permit.

CASE 11.7   Fair Treatment of Employees

Joe Sánchez has been hired as kitchen manager in a quick-service restaurant located in southern California. Because of labor shortages, it is common practice in the area to hire undocumented workers in back-of-the-house positions, such as dishwashing and groundskeeping. Because of their status, these workers do not have any recourse for protection under the law. One of Joe's many duties is to schedule all kitchen workers. His boss has specifically entrusted Joe with lowering the payroll and employee-related expenses from the current 27 percent of revenue to 24 percent, which is the goal to be reached by all the company's restaurants.

Thinking that his future promotion will depend on his present performance, Joe makes the decision to lay off six "normal" employees and replace them with six undocumented aliens. Joe wants to be fair and makes the decision to pay the new workers the minimum wage established by law. The restaurant, at the same time, will save the benefits that the company offered to "regular" employees. Joe checked with several colleagues working in other restaurants in the area and was told that none provided any benefits to undocumented workers.

Six months after the changes had been made, the restaurant labor cost percentage was under control and Joe was promoted to assistant manager in a larger store in San Francisco.

ASSIGNMENT: Discuss this case and determine whether Joe Sánchez behaved ethically in this situation.

KEY CONCEPTS/TERMS

benchmarking

business collusion

code of ethics

ethical dilemma

undocumented alien

Chapter 12

Hospitality Communication

CHAPTER OBJECTIVES

- Review the elements of the communication process.
- Discuss and practice formal presentations.
- Learn about impromptu speaking.
- Understand the importance of written communication.
- Explain the skills needed to become a good face-to-face communicator.
- Learn about body language in communication.

OVERVIEW

Proficiency in oral and written communication is considered a key skill by recruiters hiring hospitality graduates. Some hospitality business operators believe that there is a direct link between the good communication skills of their employees and high company profits. Therefore, they seek out graduates of hospitality programs who are excellent communicators. Where back-of-the-house workers may be recent immigrants or guests may come from foreign countries, recruiters appreciate job applicants' ability to speak a second language. In this chapter we look at cases that will illustrate to students the need for good verbal and written communication skills in the workplace.

THE COMMUNICATION PROCESS

Managers and supervisors spend a considerable part of their time communicating with others. In hospitality situations, managers must be capable of communicating effectively with employees, guests, vendors, and colleagues as well as with their own corporate bosses or with the community at large. Some people are better with certain types of communication situations than others: A manager who is excellent at one-on-one communication with an employee or a customer may be a lackluster speaker in the public arena. Or the reverse: A manager who is an engaging public speaker may be very poor in situations that call for a two-way exchange. In addition, a natural speaker may be an ineffective writer, or the person adept at written communication may falter with oral communication. It is imperative that a hospitality manager be competent in all areas of communication.

Often, the most important component of one-on-one communication is **listening**, a skill that is critical to determine the needs, problems, and moods of the person who is speaking. Listening is crucial for the manager communicating with an employee or guest who is angry or upset. The mere fact that the manager is listening indicates to the speaker a concern and empathy about the problem as well as the desire to fix it. Calm and interested listening is a supervisor's best tool for dissipating the anxiety of a speaker.

Oral communication is both verbal and nonverbal. **Verbal factors** are the words spoken and the tone of voice used. Because words can lead to many things—from misunderstanding and false accusations to trust and loyalty—good managers must be careful to measure what they say. In most situations, a manager's message will be taken literally by employees and may be repeated many times. A manager's **voice rate** is also important because it sets the pace of the communication. Voice conveys many feelings—from anxiety and urgency to enthusiasm, serenity, and confidence.

Nonverbal behavior also sends signals to employees. Gestures serve as expressions of emotion, and eye contact is used to establish trust in our culture. Employees from different cultural backgrounds, however, often display other nonverbal behaviors. For example, Hispanics and Native Americans may avoid eye contact with their bosses, not because they are untrustworthy but because that is their way of showing respect.

Young graduates should strive to build rapport with the staff with whom they are to communicate. **Rapport** is the ability to communicate effectively while making others comfortable during the communication process. In this way, supervisors and managers should adapt comfortable behaviors to establish good communication with their employees. Another way to establish good rapport is through **empathy**—the appreciative perception or understanding of another person.

Here are some useful tips regarding communication:

- Weigh your answers; don't shoot from the hip.
- Keep an open-door policy for employees and guests.
- Chat informally with employees whenever possible.
- Listen carefully before you are ready to answer.
- Avoid being critical; be factual instead.

CASE 12.1 Establishing Rapport

You have been hired as F&B manager of an institutional food company in Boston. Four weeks into the job, a group of workers asks to see you in your office. They want you to consider two requests: (1) to improve menus served daily in the employee cafeteria; and (2) to better maintain the eating area in and around the cafeteria, including the restrooms. Determined to solve these problems, you ask the group to give you a few days to look into them and make the necessary decisions.

A personal inspection of the employee cafeteria reveals that the area is not as clean as it could be. Specifically, the floor has not been stripped and finished for some time, the tiles on the restroom walls are spotted, the lighting is dim, and there are dark marks on all doors around the knobs. After speaking with the executive chef and sampling several dishes on the employee menu, you decide that the food is plentiful, varied, and wholesome. There is, however, a lack of fresh items, such as salads and fruit.

You plan to address the employees at a staff meeting, knowing that in this case, as in most other communication cases, establishing rapport with the audience is essential. The points to be made are these:

1. The employee cafeteria area will be deep-cleaned next week.
2. The cafeteria attendants' hours will be extended so that the eating area and restrooms are cleaned after each meal period.
3. The food served now is nutritious and well prepared.
4. A minimum of one fresh salad will be served at lunch and dinner. All canned fruit servings will be replaced by fresh fruit salad with a side of cottage cheese. Yogurts will be added to the breakfast menu.

ASSIGNMENT: Imagine that your classmates are the employees attending the staff meeting. Address the group and communicate to them your decision in a convincing, effective way.

FORMAL PRESENTATIONS

Sooner or later, hospitality graduates will be asked to present a subject to a formal gathering. Part of the hiring strategy of some companies is to ask students interviewing for a job to make a formal presentation on a topic of their choice.

Formal presentations require good preparation. Rather than memorizing a speech word for word, speakers should simply assemble and arrange ideas beforehand. A good way is for the presenter to prepare a visual aid listing the main points or facts of the presentation. This approach has two purposes: one is to divert the focus of attention of the audience to a point away from the speaker; the second is for the presenter to be able to talk about the topics listed on the screen in an orderly manner.

Formal presentations should be divided into three parts: (1) a short introduction, (2) the main body of the speech, and (3) a brief summary of the main points presented. Here are a few useful tips on delivering a presentation:

- Emphasize the main points of the presentation.
- Maintain eye contact with the audience.
- Bring the main ideas home using appropriate gestures.
- Keep an even, steady pace throughout the presentation.
- Pause briefly between topics.
- Relate topics to listeners' interests.
- Provide illustrations and examples.
- Convey the belief that you are speaking in earnest.
- Make the audience feel like a partner in the presentation.

CASE 12.2 The Formal Presentation

Angela Crosby has been appointed manager in an institutional company serving the catering needs of a school district in Georgia. After 3 months on the job, Angela believes that the company's bottom-line results could be improved substantially by investing in transportation and food-holding equipment. According to her research, the current labor cost was too high because the number of trips from the main commissary to the serving sites was excessive.

Angela's boss was receptive to her ideas and asked her to make a formal presentation to him and other corporate officials at the company's headquarters. Her goal will be to present and convey several facts to the panel:

- Currently, two small-sized vans making food deliveries to 12 schools in the district. The vans run from 4 AM to 4 PM (12 hours). The average number of trips to and from the commissary is 18 per day.
- The average monthly automotive expenses are $1,200. This includes van maintenance, gasoline, and vehicle state permits. The cost of labor for four employees is based on 8 hours per day for two full-time drivers and 4 hours per day for two part-time drivers.
- Angela's proposal is to purchase one large-sized van and the required food-holding equipment to do the same service and to reduce the driver time by one-half. Automotive expenses would also be substantially reduced by operating one vehicle instead of two.
- The initial cost of the new van would be offset by selling the two smaller vans.

ASSIGNMENT: Prepare a formal presentation to demonstrate the merit of Angela's proposal. Include visual aids and quantitative data to support the proposal.

IMPROMPTU AND EXTEMPORANEOUS SPEAKING

Giving prepared speeches can be relatively easy because the speaker can gather and organize information ahead of time. However, the ability to succeed in **impromptu speaking**—speaking without preparation—is even more difficult in some ways than the ability to speak after thorough preparation.

The demands of the hospitality business make it indispensable for managers to be capable of putting together thoughts quickly and verbalizing fluently. To obtain this ability, it is best to practice **extemporaneous speaking**—speaking on the spur of the moment without preparation or notes. Students can do this by becoming members of **Toastmasters International**— an organization that teaches speaking skills with branches throughout the United States. Students can also learn by volunteering for impromptu speaking in class or later at formal or informal gatherings when in the workplace.

CASE 12.3   Extemporaneous Speaking

As front desk manager of a resort in New Jersey, you have just checked in a large Elderhostel group on their way to Johnson and Wales University. As the guests gather in the lobby, waiting to be escorted to their rooms, the group guide raises her voice and signals for you to come forward to welcome the group. "I'd like to introduce the front office manager, Mr. Fernandez," she begins. "He's going to have a few words for you on the part of the resort."

ASSIGNMENT: Improvise some brief comments for the Elderhostel group. You may want to welcome them to the resort in the name of the general manager and briefly describe the services that the property offers.

WRITTEN COMMUNICATION

As future hospitality managers, graduating students should have developed the ability to communicate in writing effectively. Because written statements are permanent, they become lasting records that may reflect positively or negatively on the writer in future situations. Therefore, all such communication must be carefully written and made accurate. Graduates from higher education institutions are expected to be able to write correctly, observing the rules of grammar, spelling, and punctuation.

As with formal presentations, written statements should be, if possible, divided into three sections: (1) introduction, (2) main body, and (3) conclusion. The most common forms of written communication are e-mails, memorandums, and business letters.

CASE 12.4 Communication by E-mail: A Tour Guide Complaint

Tom Shaw is the general manager of a restaurant/cafeteria in Providence, Rhode Island. Terry Natali, the corporate public relations manager of Tom's company, sent him the following e-mail:

Dear Tom:

We have received a letter from the manager of Seaventure Tours regarding the visit of one of their groups to your cafeteria on July 15. According to the tour guide, they had to wait 20 minutes before they could be seated for lunch, in spite of the fact that a reservation had been made 2 months in advance. Although they found the food to be of excellent quality, they complained of the servers being curt and appearing to be stressed out. Could you please look into the matter and respond by e-mail, giving me all the facts so I can answer the letter knowledgeably. As you know, Seaventure Tours represents a good chunk of our overall business. Besides, they have been customers of ours for years and, obviously, we don't want to lose them for any reason.

Cheers, Terry

ASSIGNMENT: Answer Terry's e-mail, explaining how this incident may have occurred.

CASE 12.5 Communication by Memorandum: Exceeding Budget Expectations

The fiscal year is almost over. All indications point to your restaurant having exceeded budget expectations for the year, for which you received a letter of commendation from the regional office of your company. As manager, you believe that the success is mainly due to the stellar performance of your employees, particularly the chef, who was able to reduce the food cost percentage by five points from the budgeted projections.

You decide to let the good news be known to the entire staff by writing an internal memo and posting it on the bulletin boards of all departments.

ASSIGNMENT: Write a memo on the subject, making sure to use the appropriate format for interdepartmental memorandum communication.

CASE 12.6 Communication by Business Letter: A Luncheon Proposal

As sales manager of a hotel in downtown Toledo, Ohio, you receive the following letter:

October 31, 20_ _
Chamber of Commerce
345 Cherry Street
Toledo, OH 43551

Dear Sir:

The Chamber of Commerce plans to have its annual awards luncheon on November 20. We anticipate that between 250 and 275 members will be attending the event. We are asking all hotels in the area that can accommodate this number of people to provide us with a proposal to cater the function.

The Chamber's budget for the luncheon is $11.75 per person for a three-course meal, including gratuities. Accommodation for no-salt, kosher, and vegetarian guests must be provided. (We will announce the exact number of special requests in writing prior to the event.) We would like to receive three different menus to choose from for this occasion.

If you are interested in hosting the event, please let us know at your earliest convenience.

Sincerely,

Jake Hancock
President

ASSIGNMENT: Answer this letter, using the appropriate format for business letter writing.

FACE-TO-FACE COMMUNICATION

The amount and intensity of verbal communication that takes place in hospitality operations is substantial. Most of the communicating consists of one-on-one verbal interaction. Face-to-face discussions, formal and informal, take place with employees and guests throughout the day. In this type of direct communication, managers and supervisors have the opportunity to listen, motivate, express thanks, encourage, and, most important, gather and disseminate information. Through informal or "grapevine" communication, first-line supervisors and managers are able to learn how employees feel about the company. By listening attentively to guests, they can obtain information needed to redirect efforts or change things around to improve operations.

Regarding face-to-face communication, it is important to understand that people tend to perceive facts through the sensing system they are most comfortable with. **Visuals** are people who are comfortable mapping their perceptions in pictures; **auditories** tend to map their cognitions from sounds; **kinesthetics** are at ease perceiving facts from feelings. Managers should attempt to adapt their speech to the other person's preferred way of communication. Usually, visuals can be identified by their use of picture words such as "I see what you mean" or "Looks good to me!" Auditories use expressions such as

"I hear you" or "Sounds okay to me!" Kinesthetics use feeling words, such as "How do you feel about this?"

Language can also become a barrier between supervisors and subordinates. Because most back-of-the-house workers are recent immigrants, particularly from Central America and South America, speaking a foreign language is most needed at the supervisory level. Hospitality companies understand that hiring employees who know a foreign language is more advantageous for meeting the needs of their non-English-speaking employees and guests. It is imperative that hospitality students take foreign language courses to improve their communication skills before joining the industry.

CASE 12.7 Communication Sensing Systems

Read the following dialogue carefully:

GM:	It looks like we're having difficulties at the front desk. It appears that guests are taking too long to check out lately.
Assistant GM:	I hear you. What should we do?
GM:	How about adding a clerk on the morning shift? Do you see that as solving the problem?
Assistant GM:	That sounds good to me. But can we justify the extra expense?
GM:	Well, I can see that we might have a problem there. Perhaps we're not scheduling our guest service agents effectively.
Assistant GM:	Before we sound the alarm, let's listen to what the front office manager has to say.
GM:	Yes, let's get a clear picture of what's going on before we act. See to it immediately!

ASSIGNMENT: Identify the sensing preference of both persons. How should the assistant manager present the problem to the front office manager, whose sensing preference is visual?

BODY LANGUAGE

Besides verbal communication, the way a message is supported through non-verbal behavior affects the reactions of people toward a speaker. Nonverbal communication applies to what can be *seen* by the other person, such as gestures, facial expressions, eye contact, and positioning. For example, how you enter an office may put other people at ease or on the defensive; movement toward the front of a chair may indicate interest; mirroring of nods or smiles could indicate acceptance. Everyone knows the implications of "Be careful, the boss looks like he's in a bad mood today."

It is often said that some recruiters may decide to reject a candidate in an interview after only a few minutes of interaction. This can be caused by a negative feeling that is conveyed by a candidate's nonverbal behavior. For example, smiling is considered very important in the hospitality industry; a person who does not smile may be perceived by potential employers as overly introverted or even unfriendly, traits seen as negative by hospitality professionals.

Besides smiling, there is other positive body language that is considered important: maintaining eye contact, listening attentively (without appearing to be distracted), minimizing nervous movements (like tapping the arm of a chair or fumbling with car keys), and maintaining a relaxed body posture.

CASE 12.8   Body Language

You are presently working as the resident manager of a hotel in Philadelphia. You are also serving as president of the local Hotel/Motel Association. The city council has been announcing for some time that increasing the current lodging tax is necessary. The raise, they argue, will provide the city with extra funds to improve beautification efforts of the downtown historical areas.

The Hotel/Motel Association believes that the tax is unfair because most lodging properties in Philadelphia are not located in the downtown area. Besides, the group is convinced that the increase would serve as a deterrent to attract people to Philadelphia, negatively affecting the convention business.

In the last association meeting, you were chosen unanimously by the attending members to defend the position of the Hotel/Motel Association regarding the tax increase at next week's open forum that has been scheduled by the city.

ASSIGNMENT: Prepare the report that you will bring before the council, citing the reasons against the impending raise of the lodging tax. When you present your argument, stand in the front of the room, away from any table, chair, or lectern. Be aware of your body language.

KEY CONCEPTS/TERMS

auditories	nonverbal behavior
empathy	rapport
extemporaneous speaking	Toastmasters International
impromptu speaking	verbal factors
kinesthetics	visuals
listening	voice rate

Chapter 13

Hospitality Organizational Behavior and Management

CHAPTER OBJECTIVES

- Review the principles of hospitality company organization.
- Discuss group behavior in hospitality organizations.
- Understand the behavior of individuals in hospitality organizations.
- Review and apply the concept of productivity in the workplace.

OVERVIEW

Higher education hospitality curricula use different approaches in preparing undergraduate students to join the industry. Many programs are practical in nature, focusing on operations and skimming over the principles of organization and management theories, whereas others require specific courses on principles of management and organizational behavior. Whatever the case, employers expect hotel and restaurant management graduates to possess some knowledge of organizational and management theories and to be familiar with the application of these principles in real-life situations.

This chapter reviews the concepts of organizational behavior and the elements and functions of management, providing specific cases in which these theories can be applied. The chapter also explores the concept of labor productivity in the hospitality workplace, an issue that directly concerns hospitality managers because of the labor intensity of the industry.

COMPANY ORGANIZATION

Chances are that graduates joining hospitality companies—particularly if they join nationwide chains—will find that the organizations they will work for have been carefully planned and structured. The design of organizations is aimed at optimizing the way they operate. After joining a hospitality company, some graduates may find that the organizational structure is stable and successful. In other cases, they may be witnesses to sudden changes in structure, attempts made to improve operational results. After some time in the industry, individuals holding hotel and restaurant management degrees may (in many cases will) be compelled to restructure the organization of companies in order to maximize effectiveness. For example, if a restaurant company is not doing well, its **chief executive officer (CEO)**—the person responsible for strategy, goal setting, and policy implementation—may have to change its organizational framework by selling some stores, changing the company's concept, or eliminating one or several layers of managers or perhaps some guest services.

In all cases, changes to the current structure of a company must be weighed carefully because their effects can cause major negative consequences for employees and guests. For instance, cutting costs by eliminating a **bonus system**—monetary incentives for workers to reward productivity—may diminish the will of employees to work hard. Changes that may affect fluid communication in an organization can also constrain rather than facilitate performance. For example, if the position of assistant to the rooms division manager is eliminated in a large resort, there may be a break in communicating and translating the intentions of upper management to line employees, which may result in complaints from guests. Another example of reorganization may be a company's decision to restrict **empowerment**, a management approach that gives employees the necessary authority to provide effective customer service. For example, its line employees may no longer be able to give rebates to guests to compensate for deficient products or services. This decision could result in a large number of disgruntled guests and a decrease in return bookings.

It is important for future managers to realize that all organizational units in the workplace must be structured appropriately given the demands of the task. For instance, a restaurant serving lunch near a busy office building must provide sufficient staff to deliver this service in 45 minutes, as most office employees have only 1 hour available for lunch. At the same time, the working units must be adequately linked by good coordination and control. Besides having a sufficient number of servers and cooks to provide lunch in 1 hour, the restaurant must be organized in such a way that the service is efficient, that there is good communication between the floor and the kitchen, and that good controls are in place to ensure a profitable return.

Basically, an organizational structure consists of elements that define the goals, composition, and groupings of its units—specifically, who is accountable for each unit, how individuals and units report to others, what communication patterns are in place, who are the decision makers, and how individuals are to be rewarded or disciplined for their performance. Large hospitality companies are carefully structured to facilitate operations. Below the GM is the **executive committee**, which includes the directors in charge of divisions; each division is subdivided into departments and managed by department heads (staff); each department is grouped into supervisory units, and so on.

Recent approaches to organizational structure in hospitality operations have led to the adoption of **downsizing**, a management practice that reduces organizational layers of supervision aimed at minimizing operational costs. An example might be hiring executive housekeepers who can perform as first-line managers, without the direct intervention of the property's upper management.

CASE 13.1 Understanding Company Organization

A group of 12 independent properties in the Northwest have combined their organizational and marketing efforts under the name Hospitality Inc. The owners of each property formed the board of directors of the corporation and hired a CEO to manage the group as a sole entity. The bylaws of the company required the consensus of all members before any structural changes affecting the 12 properties could be implemented.

One year after the formation of the company, the merger has proved to be a disappointment. The CEO, Cameron Day, who had a proven successful background in sales and marketing, has not being able to bring the properties together. It appears that the 12 units remain operationally autonomous to a large extent, and are not able to cooperate with each other; in fact, they seem to be competing in most cases. The unit managers complain about the lack of corporate organization and specific operational guidelines.

Most of Cameron's efforts have been aimed at growth rather than consolidation. The result is that some of the units are not up to the service quality levels portrayed in the company's advertising. Whereas some units are luxury properties offering very good accommodations and amenities, other units are midsized establishments in need of remodeling and more efficient service. As a result, the public image of the group as a whole is poor. The better establishments are clearly disappointed because no team effort for product image and organizational purposes seems to exist.

Employee relations have also been a problem. The salaries and wages paid in some properties are lower than in others. Workers know that there are differences in the weekly take-home checks, and those who are being paid less are showing signs of discontent. Some key employees quit because they can get better wages and salaries elsewhere.

The operational aspects of the organization are also in disarray. The majority of the properties' GMs still manage their establishments their own way. Some of the "older" managers have been resisting changes proposed by the corporate office. Cameron is well aware of this situation and thinks that some managers should be asked to leave, but he decided against such a move because it would imply incurring high termination costs. Cameron has not been able to put in place a central administration strong enough to unify operational criteria.

Although there are corporate quality assurance and financial control programs in place, they are not being implemented rigorously by the units. As a result, complaints from guests are increasing by the day and administrative reports are not compiled regularly by most properties. Cameron has just learned that three properties have not conducted monthly food inventories for 2 consecutive years. The efforts of the chain to grow are not producing results. The independent operators contacted believe that the company's reputation is not sound, and they are not willing to pay a substantial management fee for services that they think will be substandard.

Of the 12 properties belonging to Hospitality Inc., five are generating a positive bottom line profit while the remaining seven are barely breaking even. Three of the less profitable units are medium-sized motels located along Interstate 5. They are old units in desperate need of being refurbished. Although the owners have been asked to begin remodeling efforts, they refuse to invest any financial resources until Hospitality Inc. turns things around and the establishments begin to make money. They feel that the management fee they pay should generate tangible positive results. Instead, they argue, the management company is asking them to sink more money in the properties.

The owner of one of the best properties believes that the problem with Hospitality Inc. is that the number of members on the governing board is too large, not allowing for fast consensus on critical decisions that could favorably impact the chain as a whole. Frequently when major changes are proposed, the board rejects them by a narrow margin. He thinks that the company needs stricter control from headquarters—specifically, a clear chain of command and functional responsibilities to be followed by all unit managers.

ASSIGNMENT: Indicate the goals of a basic organizational plan for Hospitality Inc. Suggest an organizational chart for the company, indicating the titles of key positions.

GROUP BEHAVIOR IN HOSPITALITY ORGANIZATIONS

Hospitality professionals spend most of their time at work with other people. To be able to function well in hospitality environments, managers and supervisors must understand the behavior of groups within organizations. The difficulty of interdepartmental coordination in hospitality operations is a widespread one and can have many repercussions. For example, if the reservations department is not consulted about room availabilites, the sales department may book more rooms for a convention than are available. If the executive chef is not aware of the early checkout of a large group, breakfast food production will be miscalculated because of an understaffed kitchen.

Managers must understand that groups (departments) perform tasks that could not be accomplished by individuals alone. At the same time, a group must be seen as a social entity in which individual beliefs, culture, and values must be accepted and shared by members. When this is not the case, the group's coherence usually suffers. A department supervisor in hospitality operations must see to it that there is a balance between the functions that the group is serving for the individual members and the functions the group must serve toward the organization. For example, a kitchen manager has created a department where everyone works very well with each other. This group, however, has an ongoing feud with the dining room servers, and the conflict is not contributing to the overall purpose of the operation. In other words, while members of a department should view their group as an important part of their lives and work well together, they must understand that interacting with other groups is critical for the benefit of the organization as a whole.

Basically, it is a manager's job to ensure that **output**—the productivity results of a worker or group of workers—meets or exceeds organizational standards of quantity and quality. At the same time, the manager must facilitate interaction and cooperation with other departments in the property. The existence of independent kingdoms so common in poorly run hospitality operations must be, in all cases, prevented.

There are several approaches that will foster the effectiveness of group work:

- Hiring the right person for the group in question
- Providing clear guidelines for group performance
- Instituting an effective training period to achieve group effectiveness
- Having a motivational system of rewards for good performance
- Explaining clearly to group members the disciplinary consequences resulting from unacceptable performance
- Fostering interdepartmental communication and cooperation

CASE 13.2 Departmental Coordination of Activities

Ann Taylor has been hired as executive housekeeper of a 500-room hotel located near Atlanta's Hartsfield International Airport. Ann holds a degree in hotel and restaurant management from a leading university in the discipline and has 4 years of experience in front office operations with a nationwide hotel chain. Ann's employer selected her from 43 other candidates because her academic record showed that she had done very well in an organizational behavior course in college. The recruiter thought that this qualified her for reorganizing the housekeeping department of the hotel.

Ann spent her first 2 weeks on the job looking into the department's records and having one-on-one meetings with supervisors and hourly employees. One of the major problems, she soon found out, was the high turnover and absentee rates of the department. According to the personnel department, the estimated average cost for replacing a room attendant at the hotel is $1,700. This cost includes advertising for the position, hiring and training the worker, and providing additional supervision during the induction period.

The exit interviews conducted by the human resources department have identified some of the reasons for leaving. Room attendants claim great frustration on the job as the main cause. An employee who quit recently tried to explain the problem: "Each one of us had to fend for herself. Every morning I had to scramble for linen to stock my cart. Some other housekeepers hid washcloths in their lockers to have them available when needed." Housemen complained that often they had to fight over a vacuum cleaner to have the hallways cleaned. A section housekeeper said, "I take pride in cleaning my rooms but never got a bonus while others are sloppy workers and get the same wage that I get." A room attendant with more than 5 year's work in the hotel offered this comment: "The workload of 13 rooms per one 8-hour shift is ridiculous. I could easily finish 16 rooms a day if they paid me more money. I already get 10 rooms done by lunchtime and slow down for the remaining three until it is time to clock out."

Overall morale is low among the housekeeping workers. "They treat us like dirt," said one of the housekeepers. "The front desk and maintenance people think that they can boss us around." The front desk and engineering departments in turn accused housekeeping of not being able to communicate professionally.

Ann is now faced with high absentee and turnover rates, lack of esprit de corps among workers, poor interdepartmental communication, and numerous guest complaints.

ASSIGNMENT: Specify the steps that Ann Taylor should take to reorganize the department and change for the better the internal and interdepartmental performance of housekeeping.

INDIVIDUAL BEHAVIOR OF HOSPITALITY EMPLOYEES

Besides understanding the organizational structure of companies, hospitality graduates should have a clear knowledge of how people behave within organizations and their motives for doing so. For example, some individuals prefer to perform manual rather than clerical tasks; some are professionally ambitious, wanting to move fast up the management ladder, whereas others are content to stay in the same job, performing the same work day after day. Thus, managers should develop the ability to help all workers find those positions that best suit their abilities and personal needs.

It is not uncommon to find hospitality employees, such as section housekeepers and line cooks, willingly performing repetitive work for long periods of time. Outside the United States, many servers, porters, and other hourly workers hold the same position in the same house for years, and in some cases for generations. The reason for this identification with a job is explained by the belief of psychologists that human behavior is motivated by the needs of each individual. Some of these needs may be psychological, such as the need for social status or recognition; others may be tangible, such as the need for money, good health benefits, or job security. In all cases, it should be up to the manager to provide individuals with tasks that provide them with the opportunity of achieving their preferred job-related outcomes.

CASE 13.3 Individual Working Preferences

Makul Patel has been transferred to a hotel-casino in Las Vegas as kitchen manager. Makul worked his way up to management from his initial position of dishwasher. This is his first management job after 7 years with the company.

The food and beverage director of the hotel has confided in Makul that the kitchen department is having serious personnel problems, mainly because the outgoing manager was incapable of using the workforce effectively. Makul was told that some employees felt that they were stuck in their positions for years, without having a fair chance to move up in rank or transfer to other departments. The kitchen is obviously in need of reorganization.

One of the employees in the kitchen, Eileen Coffee, had worked as breakfast cook for 15 years. A single parent with her only daughter attending college, Eileen loved her job. Although her shift began at 5:30 AM, she had never been late. Every day she looked forward to her cooking routine. Her current hourly wage was $13.50 an hour, which she considered sufficient to cover her living expenses and contribute to her daughter's college tuition fees. She believed that "for a person without a formal education, her wages were adequate, especially because the medical and dental benefits provided by the company were very good." Eileen could not think of any other work she would like to do. To her, going to the hotel every day was a joy and felt that her place of work was like home. Eileen was very proud of her performance in the kitchen, and she was highly regarded by the hotel's management and her fellow coworkers.

After starting in his new position, Makul spent a week carefully observing the way employees performed their duties in the kitchen. He made a list of what he considered deficiencies, including his determination that Eileen was not fast enough behind the line to handle the high number of food orders at the peak of the breakfast service. Eileen was getting on in years, and she was slowing down in her ability to fill orders quickly. However, there had not been any complaints from the service staff about her performance.

Makul thought that it was time to make bold changes to improve productivity in the kitchen and decided to replace Eileen with a younger, more energetic person. He swiftly transferred Eileen to the garde-manger department, refusing to listen to her plea against being changed. At first, she threatened to quit, but in the end she agreed to accept the new position, fearing that she could lose her job altogether if she refused to agree to the transfer.

ASSIGNMENT: Discuss the effect that Makul's decision could have on Eileen's behavior and her level of satisfaction from the job thereafter. Also comment on the reaction of the kitchen personnel as a group after witnessing this staff change.

HOSPITALITY MANAGEMENT

After a period of initial training, hospitality graduates are in most cases promoted to supervisory positions. The next steps up the management ladder usually involve running departments, divisions, and finally entire operational units, such as freestanding restaurants, hotels, or resorts. Once the stage of general manager has been reached, that person is ultimately responsible for keeping the entire operation functioning effectively or for integrating two or more organizational units into a working system. Thus, when hospitality graduates are promoted from operational to upper management levels, they must possess a thorough knowledge of how to formulate strategies; that is, they must be able to assess the organization internally and to appraise the external environment in which it exists. Based on the assessment, the manager must allocate appropriate resources to carry through the operational activities.

After formulating their strategies, managers must put them to work by way of clearly defined plans, goals, and objectives. Specifically, the implementation process involves four classic management functions:

1. **Planning**—setting objectives and developing strategies to achieve them.
2. **Organizing**—coordinating the internal functioning of the workplace and establishing a pattern of relationships with other operational teams.
3. **Controlling**—measuring actual standards with expected standards established during the planning process and effecting necessary corrections if deviations from the standards are found.
4. **Directing**—achieving the goals of a company or operational unit.

Besides these functions, managers must be able to interact well with subordinates and to gather and disseminate information throughout the organization. Managers who are perceived by subordinates as poor communicators usually have difficulty running organizations effectively. In all cases, good managers must be willing and able to implement change when it is needed, and in effect to view the organization as a live organism in constant need of restructuring.

Change, however, is usually resisted by groups or individuals who feel comfortable working in existing conditions. They view it as a threat to the **status quo**, the state in which anything was or is without change. Because of this, managers must create appropriate motivational conditions and foster participation in the planning and execution of change for those involved in and affected by the process.

CASE 13.4   Understanding Company Reorganization

Pineville, Arizona, is a college town with a population of 60,000 residents. The average number of students on the university campus is about 13,000. The city receives many tourists during the summer months, mostly on their way to and from the Grand Canyon National Park.

The major restaurant and lodging areas in Pineville are located along Broadway and off Interstate 40, which crosses the city east to west. A large variety of franchised and independent restaurants and bars are located here, including quick service, family, vegetarian, and ethnic eateries as well as sports, student, juice, and traditional bars and pubs. Many residents eat out regularly. College students have the choice of eating in on-campus facilities or at the large variety of restaurants and bars that the town offers. Although competition is fierce, the abundance of local customers, students, and tourists seems to provide sufficient business for most establishments to do well. On weekends, there are usually lines waiting for tables at most restaurants and student bars. Among these establishments are three restaurants owned by a local family incorporated as Ponderosa Inc.

Ponderosa Inc.

Ponderosa Inc. consists of three restaurants owned by a family who started the business in the 1960s. Paul James, the founder of the company, owned a lumber mill that went out of business after logging operations all but stopped in the region. Rather than moving out of town, he converted an old barn into a restaurant. Several years later, he purchased two new restaurants to be run by his children, John and Laurie James. Today, Paul is president of the corporation, and John and Laurie are board members. Each of the three restaurants offers a distinctive atmosphere and menu. Although all provide customers with good quality eating, one is much more successful than the other two.

The James' Restaurant   The James' Restaurant, the establishment opened by Paul James in a converted lumber barn, was the first full-service restaurant in Pineville. Over the years, it became a local landmark, renowned for its fine menu and service. Today, its clientele consists mostly of repeat customers in an older age category, families, and some business executives wanting to invite visitors from out of town to a full, leisurely meal in a nostalgic setting. The establishment also does substantial business with seasonal bus tours and banquets and functions from local profit and nonprofit organizations.

Because of the traditional nature of the restaurant, a younger market has not been pursued because Paul believes that college students do not fit in with the restaurant's clientele. As manager, he views the restaurant as a place to visit for a special evening dinner. Paul attributes the steady drop in business over the last 5 years to the intense competition created by the new restaurants in town. He insists on continuing with the quality menu and service that he has provided for the last 40 years.

The James' Restaurant consists of three connecting dining rooms, seating a total of 180 customers at any given time. The décor is rich and inviting, with nutty pine walls, oak beam ceilings, and wooden floors. Each of the dining areas can be closed to cater private banquets and functions. The cocktail lounge can serve a capacity of 60 customers and can be accessed without entering the restaurant. The dimly lit room has a large woodstove in one corner and solid darkly stained furniture placed around a small dance floor. Servers and bartenders wear distinct Western-style attire. On weekends, electronic keyboard music is played in the evening, hoping to attract younger clientele. Business at the lounge, booming in the past, is slow now, with most of the revenue coming from dining room sales.

In the restaurant, all menu items are prepared from scratch. Traditional American dishes are offered as complete dinner specials or as à la carte items, from roast duck, stuffed jumbo shrimp, and prime rib to chicken potpie. Some favorite entrees among the older clientele are surf and turf, roast leg of lamb, grilled sole, sirloin steak, lamb chops and liver and onions. Paul has made a point to set the highest standards for ingredients. Most dishes are prepared with real butter and heavy cream. Pecan rolls and corn fritters are the specialty of the house.

The Lumberjack Restaurant　The Lumberjack Restaurant, the second restaurant opened by the James family, is located in downtown Pineville. Built on the ground floor of a historic building, it has established itself as a more upscale alternative to the quick-service restaurants in the area. John James has sought a wide target market—lunch and dinner business, with live music, usually blues and jazz, offered in the evening.

The restaurant consists of a main room with a bar at one end and a stage at the other. There are 15 tables on the floor and about 70 chairs. The back connecting room offers a wide-screen TV for sports broadcasts, a pool table, and an electronic dartboard. The exposed-brick walls are decorated with large jazz and rock posters. The menu at the Lumberjack features a good selection of soups, salads, burgers, and Mexican dishes, together with $1.50 drafts during jazz or blues concerts. The place is usually packed for lunch and dinner, with customers attracted by the simple yet tasty menu at affordable prices. A $6.95 brunch on Sundays brings in families before and after church. The service is courteous and efficient, and meals are served promptly without any fuss by casually attired servers. Beer is poured in hard plastic glasses and paper napkins are used instead of napery. The Lumberjack clientele, particularly the college students, love the informality of the restaurant.

Chez James　The latest acquisition of the James group is a quality French restaurant. Since going on a trip to Europe with her high school class, Laurie James has dreamed of managing a French-style bistro. She worked diligently to obtain a degree from a culinary school and gained some experience in her father's two other restaurants when she was a teenager. Today she is directly responsible for all operations at Chez James, including food purchasing and supervising the menu. Her husband John, a native of Wales, is her assistant in charge of guest and personnel relations. He is also an expert in classic tableside dining room service and in quality wines.

Located in a quiet area of town, Chez James is the perfect place for elegant dinners accompanied by the best cocktails and select wines. Despite its good reputation, the restaurant averages only about 55 covers a day.

Advertising

Each property follows a separate advertising plan. Paul does not believe that the James' Restaurant should be advertised locally, thinking that the restaurant's reputation and word of mouth are enough to keep local customers returning. The establishment is advertised in telephone directories, and brochures are sent regularly to the town's visitor's center. It is apparent that the current advertising effort is insufficient to offset the seasonal fluctuations in business and to attract new customers.

The manager of the Lumberjack insists on advertising the restaurant everywhere. Spots on the local radio are constant when the jazz and blues bands are playing. The place is advertised in the university's weekly publication and at all sports events on campus. Food and drink specials are featured in the local newspaper and brochures are mailed frequently by an advertising company.

Chez James is listed in Host Magazine, which is placed in rooms at all lodging establishments in the area, and in the travel section of the local Sunday newspaper. To reduce operational costs, Laurie has recently discontinued advertising on two billboards and on three regional radio stations.

Organization

Paul James has been the soul of the organization since the founding of the first restaurant. Besides managing the James' Restaurant, he is the de facto decision maker for the three properties, with each manager operating independently but following the whims of the family patriarch. There is poor interproperty communication. Standard operating procedures, training methods, and employee manuals exist but are not followed consistently; everyone considers the organizational environment of the company to be "like a family."

Accounting is the only procedure that is totally integrated for the three properties. After opening Chez James, Paul hired Warren Murphy as company controller to coordinate all financial procedures. A CPA with extensive experience in the hospitality industry, Warren has done an excellent job in keeping accurate records and cash controls. In view of the declining profits of the company as a whole, he has recently recommended hiring a corporate vice president of operations to take the reins of the organization. It seems that the only way to avoid bankruptcy somewhere down the road is to implement immediate changes in the mission, organization, and management procedures of the company.

A summary of results can be seen in the operating statement shown below.

	James' Restaurant	Lumberjack	Chez James
Food sales	$72,553	$539,802	$289,771
Cost of food sales	34,825	145,746	89,829
Beverage sales	12,334	269,901	81,136
Cost of beverage sales	3,823	59,378	37,323
Gross profit	$46,239	$604,579	$243,755
Labor cost	35,652	210,522	144,654
Other expenses	5,347	47,772	22,254
Fixed expenses	7,640	89,067	77,890
Net profit	$−2,400	$257,218	$−1,043

After closely examining the year's results, Warren makes clear to the board that the Lumberjack is the only successful establishment and that operational costs of the other two restaurants are bringing the company down.

Recognizing the difficult position the company is in, the James family decides to hire a professional troubleshooter to regain financial stability for the company.

ASSIGNMENT: Imagine that after several years working in the hospitality industry you accept the position of vice president of operations with Ponderosa Inc. Prepare a plan for the reorganization of the company that integrates the mission, operations, advertising, personnel, and financial goals of the group.

PRODUCTIVITY MANAGEMENT

In the workplace **productivity** is the work output of a worker or group of workers. Although it is the result of various forces, the unit of measurement of output in hospitality operations is usually a standardized product, like the number of rooms cleaned in one 8-hour shift or the number of customers served by a server in a banquet. Thus, in general, labor productivity measures output per hour of work. Effective productivity in the workplace helps keep the business competitive and usually results in greater profits for the owners and better benefits for employees. Because hospitality is a labor-intensive industry, managers must strive to maintain productivity high at all levels of the organization. When measuring productivity, the quality factor should always be taken into account— for instance, we could clean more rooms per shift but they would be sloppily finished. In order to keep the quality factor in the equation, productivity, simply stated, could be defined as "obtaining the maximum work output with the best quality possible using the least number of work hours."

There are three basic factors that can affect productivity: (1) the workers involved, (2) the equipment used, and (3) the working methods in place. Thus, productivity can be positively or negatively affected by the individual capacity of employees and their training, by the equipment being used (if it is obsolete or in disrepair), and by the way work is performed. For example, a new house-person in the housekeeping department of a hotel will not be able to achieve high productivity if he has not been trained effectively before performing work on his own. The same houseperson will not do his work productively if the vacuum cleaner he uses needs three passes rather than one to clean the hallway carpet; in this case he will need extra time to do the job. Again, productivity will be low if the houseperson assigned to the twelfth floor in a high-rise building needs to frequently take the elevator to a storeroom in the basement to pick up equipment or supplies. The extra time wasted on unnecessary trips will lower each worker's productivity output.

Psychological and physiological factors can also affect productivity. Low morale, relationships with other workers, and abusive treatment by supervisors can negatively affect employee productivity. Poor working conditions—for example, working in a laundry room that is badly ventilated or whose average temperature is 115 degrees—can also diminish the productivity of workers. Employee productivity also decreases when workers are required to be on the job for too many hours. The hospitality industry is notorious for having employees work long hours. It is common for line employees to clock more than 60 hours per week, often with no days off, or to be scheduled evening and morning shifts back to back. Even the performance of committed employees like supervisors and line managers is eventually undermined by fatigue. In some cases persistent overwork leads to employee burnout. Although management must transform new employees into a productive workforce, they must in turn be aware of the factors limiting workers' performance.

On the other hand, high levels of productivity can be achieved by having a **reward system**, a method that ties adequate compensation to performance. Most workers want to see a direct relationship between their output and financial rewards. Managers need to look at **labor productivity**, which is the amount of labor it takes to produce a certain level of output.

CASE 13.5 Labor Productivity

The Hotel Group Inc. decided to cut the pay of its 1,400 hourly employees by 8 percent and reduce their vacation time by 15 percent to help the company avoid bankruptcy. In addition, the corporation's CEO announced the downsizing of the middle-management workforce by 10 percent; this represented a total of 70 positions companywide. The Hotel Group saw the reductions in salaries and wages as inevitable and called them "a crucial first step in saving the company from divesting itself of several properties." The next step, the CEO said, would be to focus on restructuring 60 percent of its $125 million long-term debt and on improving the company's technology infrastructure, which, according to her, was not state-of-the-art.

Conscious of the drastic reduction in manpower, management asked all employees to be ready to work 6-day weeks during periods of high occupancy and to put in the necessary hours daily to provide adequate service to guests.

ASSIGNMENT: Consider the decisions made by the Hotel Group Inc. affecting the workforce and predict the impact they will have on employee productivity. If you were company CEO and believed these actions were absolutely necessary to save the company, how would you put them into effect? Present a plan of action for their implementation.

KEY CONCEPTS/TERMS

bonus system
chief executive officer (CEO)
controlling
directing
downsizing
empowerment
executive committee

labor productivity
organizing
output
planning
productivity
reward system
status quo

Chapter 14

Hospitality Leadership

CHAPTER OBJECTIVES

- Review the traits, skills, and personal characteristics of leaders.
- Discuss the leadership behavior of successful managers.
- Review the leadership styles of managers.
- Describe the types of leadership power.
- Explain the concept of situational leadership.
- Understand the need for managers to be politically correct.

OVERVIEW

Hospitality companies actively look for graduating seniors who show signs of having the necessary ability to lead. For this reason, students about to be interviewed for jobs should clearly understand the concept of leadership, its nature and its importance. Company recruiters are trained to identify the traits and characteristics of potential leaders; they are aware that technical skills alone are not sufficient for success. Additional factors—for example, developing leadership styles and the ability to match a particular style to a specific situation, knowing when to delegate and how to motivate and empower subordinates, and understanding political strategies in the workplace—can be developed over time while on the job. If it is true that certain leadership traits are inherent in individuals, it is also true that a mature leadership behavior and style can be achieved only after several years of working with people and organizations. The success that graduates will have in their careers will depend on their ability to be effective leaders.

THE TRAITS, SKILLS, AND CHARACTERISTICS OF LEADERS

One of the overall goals of hospitality programs is to prepare students for administrative positions, or management. Most of the courses taught emphasize four key functions: planning, organizing, controlling, and directing. While the first three are basically administrative, the function of directing deals with leading others and understanding the vision and interpersonal aspects of a manager's job. Specifically, the directing function has to do with influencing, motivating, and energizing people to work to their potential, and with the ability to implement change effectively. The administrative and leadership roles of managers cannot survive if they are not both managed and executed efficiently. A hospitality company that is administered perfectly will not excel if it does not operate under a vision of what the organization can become in the future. In addition, if the employees in a company are not motivated to function as a team and to cooperate with each other, the organization may languish to the point of extinction. In other words, the long-term outcome of having a company run by indifferent employees is usually mediocrity. For example, although most franchised restaurants are similar in décor, follow the same procedures, and offer the same menu, some are very successful operations while others barely make the mark. Often, the difference has to do with leaders who are able to inspire other employees. There is a "feel" to well-run restaurants, a special atmosphere that pervades the place. In a hospitality establishment with an effective manager, the servers will go out of their way to be helpful, determined to provide efficient friendly service and to please their manager.

Personality is obviously a key component of leadership. Several characteristics have been identified as indicators of an effective leadership personality, although no set of traits have been recognized that absolutely predict success or failure. The following characteristics of successful leaders are most frequently noted:

- Achievement oriented
- Adaptable to situations
- Assertive
- Attentive to detail
- Cooperative
- Decisive
- Dominant in influencing others
- Emotionally stable
- Enthusiastic
- Fairminded
- Persistent
- Tolerant of frustration
- Tolerant of stress
- Willing to assume responsibility

Certain skills are also essential for successful leaders:

- The ability to conceptualize data and goals
- The use of creativity in all facets of the workplace

- Fairness in dealing with staff and competitors
- Good communication with all levels of staff
- The ability to persuade others
- Socially oriented
- The use of tact in dealing with others

Certain weaknesses must be avoided by managers in leadership roles:

- Arrogance
- Insensitivity to others
- Inability to delegate (micromanaging)
- Obstinacy about people or situations
- Dishonesty

Many of the key components of leadership style are related to physical endurance, education, and industry experience. To perform well in hospitality operational settings, managers must possess considerable energy and stamina. In most cases, hoteliers are expected to work long hours, particularly at the beginning of their careers. They are also most likely to be working when everyone else is not, particularly on evenings, holidays, and weekends, the hospitality industry's busiest times. A sound educational background is also perceived as a key leadership component by recruiting companies. Graduates from well-recognized institutions are preferred because organizations can assume they will have the necessary academic preparation for leadership roles. Industry experience is also desirable, especially if the candidate has been involved in leading subordinates effectively in successful projects.

CASE 14.1   Leadership Traits and Skills

Michael Vernon is a 36-year-old graduate from a higher-education hospitality administration program. He is married, with two children. His wife Cathy has a part-time bookkeeping job with a local department store. Michael graduated in the top one-third of his class, in spite of the fact that he was working an average of 25 hours a week as night auditor in a local motel. At the same time, he found time to participate in his community's Big Brothers and Sisters program mentoring a sixth grader from a local school.

When Michael is asked about his education, he admits that the courses he liked least were those involving technical skills, such as commercial food preparation or dining room service; he much preferred business topics such as accounting and finance. The liberal arts course he enjoyed studying most was history, mainly because he could learn the subject on his own without having to depend on others for group research and projects.

During his senior year, Michael Vernon decided that he wanted to pursue the hotel business as a career, specifically to plan, organize, and control lodging operations. He didn't think he was capable of working in the restaurant segment of the industry; he thought there were too many loose ends in these types of job for him to be in total control.

On joining the Magean Corporation, Michael was trained as front office assistant manager for the first 6 months. His previous experience as night auditor helped him design several new ways to improve operations, which resulted in substantial savings in time for balancing the audit. This provided the night clerk with extra time to prepare the morning shift work. From the front desk, Michael was rotated to the sales, banquets, and housekeeping departments.

After 7 years with the company, Michael was promoted to general manager of one of the chain's small residential hotels. Although he was initially disappointed that his first management position was in an 80-room property, he thought that the job would provide him with the necessary experience for future promotions. After managing the small unit for 4 years, Michael thought that his time to manage a large establishment had finally arrived when he learned that the company was opening two first-class resorts in California. This, however, was not to be the case. Three weeks after applying for one of the two GM positions, he was notified by the vice president of operations that the only opening to which he could be transferred was that of controller. His boss made very clear to him that his analytical skills and operational background qualified him for this position but not for that of general manager of a large property. Nevertheless, he emphasized that he would receive a substantial raise in salary if he accepted the job.

Disappointed and upset by the decision of his boss, Michael gave 3 months' notice and began looking for other opportunities. He eventually became owner-operator of a large restaurant that soon failed. Today Michael is working as accountant in a large manufacturing company where his work is much valued by his supervisor.

When Michael Vernon left the hospitality industry, the confidential file shown below was left in the office of the vice president of operations.

July 1994	Good academic record. Completed degree with honors while working 25 hours per week. Involved in community work (Big Brothers and Sisters). Some industry experience as night auditor. Hired after two successful interviews.
January 1995	Completed 6 months as manager in training in the front office. Excellent analytical skills. Suggested ways to improve night auditing procedures. Was counseled twice for receiving complaints for being unsympathetic to guest requests.
October 1997	Promoted to assistant manager in the sales department. Kept excellent records of contacts and follow-up with meeting planners. Booked several substantial pieces of

business. The sales director reported that he was talking down to a sales associate.

November 1998	Transferred to the banquets department as shift supervisor. Worked long hours when required. Good organizer. Devised liquor sales control that resulted in lowering the beverage cost percentage an average of 3 points. Several complaints were made by hourly workers about his overzealous behavior under pressure. Unable to delegate small tasks.
March 1999	Promoted to assistant executive housekeeper. Designed operating procedures for the laundry room that resulted in labor cost savings.
October 1999	Recognized as employee of the month. Instrumental in the refurbishing of 200 guest rooms. Under his supervision, the remodeling was accomplished without a glitch.
July 2000	Promoted to rooms division director. Created guidelines for departmental communication (housekeeping, front office, engineering). Fired the executive housekeeper without notice, resulting in a labor dispute settled by the company at a cost of $37,500.
October 2001	Promoted to GM of the Clarence House. Structured operational procedures and code of conduct for all departments. Ran a tight house, improving the bottom line by 5 percentage points (from 17 to 22 percent profit). The hotel lost three long-time middle managers who quit because of personality incompatibility with GM.
November 2003	Offered the position of controller at the company's new flagship property in California. Declined the offer. Submitted resignation in December 2003.

ASSIGNMENT: Identify the leadership traits and skills of Michael Vernon. How might he have been more successful in his hospitality career?

LEADERSHIP BEHAVIOR

Besides effective traits and skills, leaders must possess the right attitude to facilitate the attainment of desired goals from subordinates. For example, managers who have excellent leadership traits and skills may have certain predispositions about production and people. Leaders who want to increase productivity at all costs but are perceived as martinets by subordinates will have difficulty in attaining their goals. In contrast, leaders who take special care of their people but do not maximize the production potential of the workforce will be seen as ineffective by upper management.

The leadership behavior of managers when directing activities of a group of subordinates must be directed to put into place well-defined organizational patterns (management) while establishing effective channels of communication (leadership). The communication must be indicative of respect, mutual trust, and friendly relationships between leader and subordinates. In other words, although leaders must require employees to follow standard rules and regulations to achieve optimal production, they must also be approachable and friendly, and find time to listen to individuals. Thus, a leader should have an orientation that emphasizes production while stressing the relationship aspects of the job.

CASE 14.2   Concern for Production and for People

Holger Kjajic was hired as CEO of Jenro Hotels and Resorts, the hope being that he would be able to engineer a financial turnaround for the company. The firm's top position had been vacant since the board decided to fire Ulrich Marxen, who had been with the corporation for 15 years. A good professional, Marxen had successfully guided Jenro under the banner of "excellence in service." At the time of Ulrich's dismissal, operations at all units were being well managed and the morale of the workforce was excellent. However, according to the board, Ulrich had not been able to predict the current economic recession and to make the necessary adjustment at the time it hit the industry. As a result, the labor costs/revenue ratios had skyrocketed, and the company was desperate for cash. The board had allowed Marxen to max out bank borrowing, hoping that the economy would improve, but this did not happen.

Holger's background was in the manufacturing industry where he had the reputation of turning around companies through downsizing methods. His results had been astounding, having reduced the payroll of three large companies from 40 to 25 percent on average. A good leader, he usually got his staff to accept his management techniques as the only solution to save the companies.

Holger's detailed analyses of all Jenro's properties indicated that, as the board already knew, payroll was the main cause of the company's downturn. He immediately designed a two-prong plan of action: (1) to eliminate most of the middle managers in all departments and (2) to reduce the number of hourly employees by retraining and investing in technology. He argued that the intensive training of fewer staff would maintain current productivity and that many positions could be eliminated by installing cutting-edge computerized systems, particularly at the front desk, the controller's office, and food and beverage outlets.

The reaction from the middle managers and hourly employees being targeted for termination was quick to come. They pleaded for their jobs, many of which had been held for years. Holger's response was to stick to his long-range strategy of improving the bottom line by downsizing operations. Those employees who stayed became insecure about their jobs. In time, productivity declined sharply, communication between departments all but collapsed, and superior service to guests, for which Jenro was well known, floundered.

Two years after Holger's arrival as CEO, Jenro Hotels and Resorts filed for bankruptcy. Although operational results had been slashed by drastically reducing the number of employees, room occupancy and food and beverage revenues declined sharply. Employees blamed the loss of clientele on the deterioration of service to guests. Holger resigned from Jenro and rejoined the manufacturing industry.

ASSIGNMENT: What leadership behavior did Holger Kjajic demonstrate as Jenro's CEO? Discuss the case and propose an effective behavior pattern that should have been followed by Holger to turn around the company effectively.

LEADERSHIP STYLE

In their exercise of the "directing" function, most managers tend to have a preferred leadership style by displaying patterns of behavior that characterize them as a particular type of leader. While some allow employees latitude to express their working preferences, others provide little room for practicing innovative behavior.

Experience, education, and training help leaders to develop their style over a period of time. For example, hospitality managers trained overseas who start work in the United States often display an autocratic management style that in most cases clashes with the expectations of American workers. In contrast, managers trained in the United States who are working abroad are usually seen as too democratic in style to effectively supervise a workforce that is trained to follow orders exactly as given by the boss. One of the factors that influences leadership style is the level of confidence that managers have in subordinates; that is, the amount of control managers decide to exert on workers depends on whether they believe that people in line positions must be closely monitored or whether they should be given enough latitude to be creative in the performance of their jobs.

Leaders must learn how they come across to subordinates. If managers are perceived as being hard-nosed and controlling, they should change their style, providing capable subordinates with more room to perform their work. This is particularly important in order to avoid the perception that a manager is seeking tight behavior control, an approach that will alienate subordinates and greatly diminish the effectiveness of the leader.

Several leadership styles may be exhibited by managers, all of them summarized in terms of the degree of involvement that subordinates are allowed to have in the management function. In the **autocratic style**, leaders make decisions alone, with little or no input from subordinates. For example, an autocratic leader may decide to raise room rates unilaterally without any feedback from the sales manager. Regardless of whether this decision is right or wrong, the input from sales is essential because the sales department is aware of price trends in the area, levels of bookings on hand, and rates being charged by the competition. In the **participative style**, managers prefer to get ideas and suggestions from subordinates. In the **consultative style**, managers consult with subordinates but then make decisions by themselves. In the **democratic style**, feedback is received and subordinates are involved in the decision making process. In the **laissez-faire style**, managers allow subordinates to make work decisions and solve operational problems by themselves. This type of management style results in **empowerment**, an approach that gives employees the necessary authority to increase productivity and facilitate guest satisfaction. **Total quality management (TQM)** is a closely related theory that empowers employees to determine the best way to satisfy customers—for example, by giving a coffee shop supervisor or cashier the authority to write off bill charges for items that a guest finds to be unsatisfactory.

CASE 14.3 The Development of Leadership Style

Nels Olivas is the general manager of a Best Western motel near Colorado Springs, Colorado. For 20 years, he has been moving up the ranks to achieve his dream of becoming GM of a hospitality operation. He still remembers when he started working as a dishwasher in a large resort while attending high school. Nels waited patiently for his opportunity while other colleagues who had a college education were promoted to department heads or to upper management positions. Now that his turn had come, he was determined to show that he too could be a good manager and leader.

Nels began his tenure as GM by attending most department meetings. He took such opportunities to assure employees that he was all for empowering all workers so that they could make on-the-spot decisions regarding customer satisfaction. "I trust that each and every one of you," he usually said, "will use your judgment in making our guests feel totally at home. We don't ever want to see an unhappy customer."

On the first audit conducted by the company's corporate financial controller a year later, all accounting records were found to be faultless except for those under the category of "adjustments and rebates" in both the rooms and F&B departments. Here, the average percentage to sales was double that of the ratios shown in the statements of other company properties. The auditor's report ended with a request for the GM to make an effort to curb these results for the next accounting cycle. At the same time, the corporate office was delighted to see that guest and employee satisfaction at the motel managed by Nels had been very high. Only a few customer complaints had been sent to headquarters against the motel. Nels received a letter of commendation signed by the vice president of operations.

Nels was nevertheless disappointed that the auditor's report had not been flawless and decided there and then to put a stop to the adjustments to bills made by cashiers and supervisors at the front desk and food and beverage outlets. He issued a memo prohibiting any rebate without his own personal approval and signature under the penalty of employees being written up for any transgression of this new regulation.

One year passed and the audit was again conducted by the company's controller. The report came back perfect this time; the percent for the concept of "adjustments and rebates" had been reduced to 0.01 of total sales, a ratio never seen by the corporate accounting department before. However, despite these positive results, Nels received a stern letter from headquarters. The number of guest complaints had increased drastically last year, and several customers stated that they would never return to the motel. Overall, the occupancy rate had declined sharply from the year before. In addition, employees had also complained directly to the corporate director of human resources about lack of trust between management and employees and the absence of any latitude to make decisions on the spot to satisfy unhappy guests. Some of the letters stated that when the GM was not on the premises, line supervisors and cashiers were not able to write off charges for deficient services received by customers.

ASSIGNMENT: Discuss the case and characterize Nels Olivas's leadership style before and after the memo on adjustments and rebates. How effective do you think his leadership style had been prior to and after writing the memo? How would you have solved the problem?

LEADERSHIP POWER

Leadership power can be defined as the potential a manager has to influence others. There are several types of power that will enable a leader to gain compliance from subordinates. **Position power** enables managers to use their position in an organization to influence employees. Managers who influence workers using their behavior and personality have **personal power**. Examples of position and personal power are easily found: A line cook asks a kitchen chef why margarine is now being substituted for butter in the muffin recipe. The chef replies curtly: "Because I want it that way and I am the boss around here." In another scenario, a chef explains to a line cook that he has decided to replace margarine with butter because he wants to enhance the taste of the muffins. In the first case, the cook will comply with the chef's decision reluctantly; in the second, the cook will be influenced by the chef's positive attitude and will therefore comply willingly. Leaders who understand how to use power effectively are able to influence others more successfully than those who do not.

Position power can be subdivided into **coercive power** and **reward power**. A leader can coerce a subordinate to perform a task under the threat of a negative performance review; or the leader can persuade a subordinate by offering to give something in return. Both types of position power are closely tied with personal power, which motivates followers to trust and rely on a leader because they see their goals as being the same as those of the person they follow. Both position and personal power are necessary to lead an organization. Although in some cases leaders have to provide rewards and sanctions, in others they will have to establish rapport with followers so that they too feel integrated in the process of achieving the goals of the organization.

The coercive power of leaders can quickly be eroded if they continuously threaten subordinates with disciplinary action but seldom deliver the punishment. Reward power can also be lost if leaders give some reward to all employees whether they perform at the same level of efficiency or not and when subordinates expect compensation for any extra effort put in their job. Personal power can be lost when followers perceive the leader as dishonest or following an agenda contrary to the common interests of all involved.

CASE 14.4 Power and Leadership

Ricardo Valdez was a successful quick-service restaurant manager in Toledo, Ohio. One of the reasons for his commendable achievements as a leader was the system of rewards that he had put in place to compensate employee performance. He had established a bonus scale that was tied to a point system in which workers received extra money for good performance—for example, arriving to work on time, lack of absenteeism, going the extra step to service guests, suggesting ways to improve operations, and higher-than-average productivity. Employees worked very hard to obtain points that translated into extra cash over their minimum wages at the end of the pay period. Ricardo had demonstrated to his superiors that the bonus system in place was well worth the high productivity achieved, the better-than-average employee retention, and the achievement of superior customer service. In fact, the profit percentage of his restaurant was the highest of all the company's stores. Considered to be a star, Ricardo was asked to manage a larger restaurant that the company was opening in Columbus. Ricardo accepted and was transferred with a substantial raise in salary.

A new manager was quickly hired to replace Ricardo. Although relatively new in the industry, Jay Kung held a degree from a hotel and restaurant management program and was proud of having finished his academic work with a 3.7 GPA in his major. On taking over the management of the restaurant, Jay was surprised to find in place the bonus/compensation system initiated by Ricardo. He remembered from his college courses that rewards could be used with employees in some occasions but that this type of management power was likely to erode if workers expected to be rewarded for any extra effort put in their jobs. He decided to get rid of the system and replace it with a more equitable way of rewarding performance.

Knowing that it would be difficult to take away a recompense system that had been in place for a long period, Jay decided to increase employee wages across the board before eliminating the bonus/performance method. His goal was to motivate employees to put extra effort in their work by paying them a better wage.

Three months into the implementation of his plan, Jay Kung realized that his system had failed; productivity was down, absenteeism was up, and customer satisfaction had deteriorated to dangerous levels. Jay was flabbergasted, wondering what had gone wrong in the process.

ASSIGNMENT: Discuss this case and determine how leadership power was used by the two managers. In your opinion, who was a better administrator of power, Jay Kung or Ricardo Valdez? Explain what you would have done if you had replaced Ricardo as a manager. Determine what Jay should do after finding out that his changes had not worked as he expected.

SITUATIONAL LEADERSHIP

All managers should be capable of displaying situational leadership—applying the appropriate leadership style to each situation. For instance, it is clear that a leader should not exercise a consultative leadership style in an emergency situation. Obviously there would not be sufficient time to elicit the feedback of subordinates. At the same time, an authoritarian style should not be used when a leader is dealing with a responsible, efficient, cooperative workforce. Generally, leaders who prefer to exert a tight control in operations tend to be authoritarians, whereas those who like teamwork and give followers freedom in the exercise of their work tend to be democratic.

Besides adapting their behavior to situations, leaders should have the ability to apply different leadership styles according to the ability of subordinates to perform a certain task. For example, a manager who insists on giving orders to an employee who has been doing his work effectively for years is wasting everyone's time, whereas a manager who does not provide adequate training for new employees is not meeting expectations. Thus, leaders should be flexible in treating their subordinates according to their individual needs.

The key to understanding leadership power is to know that there is no best way to influence people; instead different types of power should be used depending on each situation and the ability and willingness of individuals to accomplish a task. A strong directive management style is needed if an employee is unable or unwilling to perform, whereas a loose style works best with willing and able workers.

CASE 14.5 Adapting Leadership Style to the Situation at Hand

Julie Largent was hired by a restaurant company after three successful interviews during her senior year in a hotel and restaurant management program. The need for supervisors in the company was extreme and she was assigned to the position of shift manager after 2 weeks of initial training. While managing her restaurant on a Sunday morning, she received a call from the dishwasher scheduled to work that day. He explained that he was having car trouble and that it would take him 2 or 3 hours to get to work. Brunch business at the restaurant was brisk and soiled items were piling up quickly in the dishwasher area. Servers were running out of clean china and flatware to reset the tables.

Julie understood that someone needed to start washing dishes immediately. She asked Genelle, a busperson, to start the machine and take charge of the washing. Genelle refused, arguing that she didn't know how to operate the dishwasher and that it was not her job to wash anything. In a panic, Julie begged the kitchen supervisor to ask a line cook to wash the pile of dirty dishes. He refused, explaining that the line was too busy and that it was not in a line cook's job description to wash dishes.

At that point, the manager remembered the emphasis that most of her college professors put on treating employees nicely. Specifically, she recalled that the main leadership premise was to influence the activities of subordinates to *willingly* accomplish goals and that a leader must be concerned about tasks *and* human relations. Her solution was to solve the problem by abandoning the serving area and washing the soiled dishes herself. Three hours later, the dishwasher arrived and took over the job.

On returning to the front of the house, she was handed four written complaints from guests about poor service. The cashier informed Julie that there was a shortage of $26 in the cash register and that two tables had walked out without paying the bill. Julie began to wonder if she had made the right decision by abandoning the supervision of the service area to wash the dishes herself.

ASSIGNMENT: How would you judge Julie Largent's leadership role in that specific situation? How effective do you think her leadership approach will be in the long run? How would you have dealt with this situation?

THE POLITICAL BEHAVIOR OF MANAGERS

Most individuals on the management track of business organizations seek to position themselves in the power ladder by exercising certain corporate political behaviors. Typically, these individuals direct their efforts to obtain the necessary influence to help them in their struggle to the top echelons of management. However, whereas some people are successful in the world of corporate power politics, others adopt questionable standards of performance. For example, building relationships and practicing networking are well-accepted, effective political moves, but manipulating others for personal gain, backstabbing coworkers, and behaving arrogantly are negative, unacceptable political behaviors.

Graduates about to join the hospitality industry for the first time should understand that their business careers may depend on building positive relationships with superiors as well as subordinates. Negative behaviors such as criticizing people, showing disloyalty to others, and behaving arrogantly will be perceived by others as devious tactics that work against career advancement and personal success.

CASE 14.6 Burning Bridges on the Management Track

Graduating with a 4.0 GPA, Jay Lowden was asked to deliver a speech at commencement, and to be the standard-bearer for his graduating class. Everyone who knew Jay assumed that his future success in the hospitality industry was a sure thing. Predictably, he obtained a manager-trainee position with Tucan Hotels and Resorts, a lodging management company operating 12 first-rate properties in northern California.

After 1 year with the organization, Jay was promoted to resident manager and promised a GM position within 2 years. After 3 years passed without his being promoted, he decided to discuss the issue with the director of personnel, Tony Favorini. The meeting did not go well at all; it ended with Jay accusing management of false promises and lack of integrity. Jay left the room in a fury, shutting the door with a loud bang. Two hours later, having cleaned up his office, he threw his working keys on Tony's desk and left the hotel for good.

It was not difficult for him to find a new job. The new company, although small, was acquiring properties at a steady pace. He was hired to manage the rooms division of a busy 350-room hotel near Sacramento. Jay's performance in the organization was so efficient that in a short time he was selected for promotion to the position of general manager of the company's flagship property in San Francisco.

At that time, the board of directors of the organization approved the takeover of the company by Tucan Hotels and Resorts, where Tony Favorini had been promoted to CEO. By executive order, Jay Lowden's promotion to GM was swiftly rescinded. In a confidential report, Tony explained to the board that he found the personal behavior of Jay Lowden to be dysfunctional.

ASSIGNMENT: What political mistake did Jay Lowden make? In your opinion, how could Jay have avoided his political blunders?

KEY CONCEPTS/TERMS

autocratic style	leadership power
coercive power	participative style
consultative style	personal power
democratic style	position power
empowerment	reward power
laissez-faire style	total quality management

Chapter 15

Hospitality Law

CHAPTER OBJECTIVES

- Review the basis of the U.S. legal system.
- Discuss the civil and legal rights of travelers and innkeepers.
- Understand the hospitality implications of contract law.
- Explain the principles of negligence as they apply to the hospitality industry.
- Discuss liability as it applies to the operation of restaurant and bars.
- Review the laws and regulations affecting employment.
- Understand the laws on discrimination in the workplace.
- Explain the work eligibility of job applicants.

OVERVIEW

Graduates of hotel and restaurant management programs must have some idea of how the legal system works in the United States as well as an understanding of the basic principles of law regarding the hospitality industry. Industry-specific laws bear on the various segments of the field and apply to many aspects of litigation, such as those pertaining to guests' and operators' legal rights, contracts, negligence, labor, and government statutes. Although it is advisable for managers to seek legal advice in all cases, some knowledge of the law can prevent them from acts that can cause grave damage to corporations.

This chapter reviews the underpinnings of the U.S. legal system, discusses the legal rights of travelers and innkeepers, and summarizes the laws and regulations affecting employment in the hospitality industry. The cases presented here are based on actual court cases.

THE U.S. LEGAL SYSTEM

There are four main types of law in the United States: (1) constitutional law, (2) statutory law, (3) common law, and (4) administrative law. That part of U.S. law that emanates from the Constitution is categorized as **constitutional law**. The fundamental principles of the Constitution determine individual rights, such as equal protection, freedom of speech and religion, and the right to due process. The laws promulgated by legislators and endorsed by executives (from president to state governors and city mayors) are called **statutory laws**. Federal and state laws are called **statutes** and local laws are called **ordinances**.

The legal rules based on previous court decisions, customs, and practices are called **common law**. These laws are constantly modified as legal decisions are made over time. The court decisions that constitute the basis for future cases are called **precedents**.

Graduates hired to work in foreign countries will find that the sources of law abroad are different from those in the United States. For example, the laws in Latin America and in several European countries are based on the Code Napoléon, the French civil code of laws introduced in the nineteenth century by Napoléon Bonaparte. This code is also the foundation of the code of the state of Louisiana, a former French colony.

Some government agencies are authorized to adopt regulations known as **administrative law**. These laws are relevant to the trade they represent. For instance, the Consumer Product Safety Commission can enact policies for the safety of consumers; the Food and Drug Administration can adopt policies to ensure the safety of foods and pharmaceutical products; OSHA can control the safety of employees in the workplace, and so on.

Civil and Criminal Law

U.S. law is classified as either civil or criminal. **Civil law** is usually applied in cases involving wrongs done to individuals. In a civil suit, compensation is sought for a **tort**—a wrongful act committed by a person that injures another. In the title of a civil case, for example, *John Lee v. Hotel Corporation*, the **plaintiff**—the wronged party who brings suit in a court of law—comes first; the **defendant**—the person or entity accused is second. In this example, John Lee is suing Hotel Corporation. Typical civil law cases involve issues such as **breach of contract**, negligence to provide reasonable care, and **fraud**.

Criminal law usually applies to cases where a wrong is committed against society (the people) for having violated a criminal statute. A criminal case seeks to punish the guilty party for wrongs such as theft and assault.

The following two examples of law cases are typical of those related to the hospitality industry:

1. A hotel is sued by a guest who slipped and fell in the bathtub. This would be classified as a civil case in which the judge may conclude

that there was (or that there was not) negligence on the part of the establishment.

2. A guest is injured by a thief trying to steal her belongings. This would be classified as a criminal case in which the jury would most likely find the defendant guilty of assault and theft.

THE CIVIL AND LEGAL RIGHTS OF TRAVELERS

Hospitality establishments are places that travelers need to use for lodging and eating, and it is therefore the business of hospitality operators to provide service to all travelers. This common law practice of old was reasserted by the Civil Rights Act of 1964, which determined that the Constitution grants all individuals the right of freedom of contract and that protects travelers against **discrimination**—differentiating in favor or against a person because of race, religion, gender, or age. Subsequently, the Civil Rights Act was extended to cover disabled guests. In 1991, the **Americans with Disabilities Act (ADA)** mandated the elimination of discrimination against individuals with disabilities. It is therefore, illegal to refuse service on the basis of disability, for example, to a person in a wheelchair. Because a goal of the act is to ensure that goods and services are provided to disabled persons, hospitality establishments must adjust their facilities to accommodate people with disabilities—for example, by providing bathrooms that can be accessed by guests in wheelchairs.

The law also protects the privacy of guests. For instance, the management of a hospitality establishment cannot consent to a search by the police of a guest's room without a warrant nor does it have a legal right to disclose phone calls made by a guest without proper legal process.

Owners of hospitality properties, however, can reserve the right to refuse service, for example, in cases of disorderly conduct, inappropriate attire, breaking a nonsmoking regulation, or being underage. Hotel operators can request police assistance to remove individuals who have been asked to leave the premises on sufficient grounds. Private clubs that are not places of public entertainment can limit attendance to members and their guests.

THE RIGHTS OF INNKEEPERS

Although guests have a right to privacy, an innkeeper has the prerogative of being in control of the establishment's rooms. For example, management has the right to move a guest to a new room for reasonable cause or the right to enter a room in case of an emergency.

The innkeeper also has the right to evict guests for nonpayment of rooms or services, for misconduct, and for overstaying an agreed time limit. Management cannot use force to eject guests but can resort to **lock out**—the act of preventing access to a room while the occupier is away—until a settlement is reached.

CASE 15.1   Exclusion of a Guest from Premises

A guest checked into a hotel, paying in advance for her board and lodging for a week at a time. After 1 month, the proprietor of the establishment removed her belongings in a proper manner and notified her that she no longer had a room at the hotel. The guest asked why she was forced to leave, and the owner answered that no explanation was due as to why. Alleging humiliation by the conduct of the proprietor, the plaintiff filed a civil suit against the owner of the inn to recover damages.

In court, the owner gave the reason that the plaintiff had been a prostitute before she came to the inn. He further stated that several female guests in the hotel were upset by the presence of the plaintiff, threatening to leave if she stayed. The plaintiff answered that, in spite of any right the hotel may have had to remove her, she had been insulted and had suffered indignity because of the manner in which she was removed. The innkeeper insisted that the presence of the expelled guest would have injured his business.

ASSIGNMENT: Discuss this case and decide whether or not the owner infringed on the legal rights of the plaintiff. What do you think was the decision of the judge? How would you have handled this situation?

CONTRACT LAW

Hospitality companies are involved in closing agreements with different parties such as guests, employees, and purveyors. When travelers make reservations to rent rooms, they agree to pay for the accommodations, and the property agrees to have the rooms available at their arrival; this constitutes a contract. A written contract is usually closed between establishments and meeting planners booking a block of rooms as well as functions for a meeting or convention.

When there is a failure to perform as agreed by the parties in a contract, a breach of contract occurs in which the nonbreaching party may decide to file a civil suit for **compensatory damages**—a sum of money to cover the loss experienced by a plaintiff. Any sum awarded to a nonbreaching party in excess of compensatory damages is called **punitive damages**. Punitive damages are awarded to plaintiffs as a punishment to the defendant for knowingly or willfully having malicious intent or actions.

Overbooking by lodging establishments often leads to breach of a reservation contract. This occurs when the property fails to honor a confirmed reservation. Travelers with a confirmed reservation who are denied a room because the hotel has overbooked are entitled to receive compensatory damages for expenses resulting from finding alternative accommodations. For this reason, hospitality establishments should assist the traveler in finding a room in another hotel. Commonly, hotels that send travelers with confirmed reservations to another house pay for transportation and a one-night stay as a gesture of goodwill. On the other hand, if the contract to rent a room is breached by a guest who has made a guaranteed reservation, he or she is liable to pay the price if the hotel is unable to relet the room.

CASE 15.2   Overbooking

A traveler made a reservation 4 months in advance in a hotel in Indianapolis to attend the Indianapolis 500 race, paying in full in advance for the reserved rooms. Two months later, the plaintiff cancelled the reservation and requested the return of his advanced payment. The hotel refused, and the plaintiff brought action, alleging that the establishment relet the rooms and was not harmed by the cancellation. This statement was supported by the fact that the Indianapolis 500 has the largest attendance of any single one-day sporting event of this type in the world.

ASSIGNMENT: Discuss this case and comment on whether or not the hotel should have returned the deposit in full. What would you have done as manager of the hotel? In your opinion, was there a breach of contract in this case?

NEGLIGENCE

When a hospitality company commits an act of carelessness that causes harm to individuals, it is considered to be **negligence**. For example, if a woman falls in the lobby of a hotel because of a missing floor tile, it would be negligence on the part of the property; if the same woman falls because the heel of her shoe broke apart, it would most likely not be a negligent act committed by the hotel.

For a defendant establishment to be liable for negligence, it must breach the duty of acting reasonably. In the case of the missing tile, the hotel breached the duty of replacing the tile to prevent a possible fall. Hospitality establishments owe duty of care for the safety of people using the property as guests or as visitors of guests, employees, and, in some cases, even trespassers. In general, this establishment might be found guilty of negligence under the following circumstances:

1. An injury was caused by an accident that would not normally have happened without negligence (failing to replace the missing tile).
2. Replacing the missing tile was within the control of the defendant.
3. Plaintiff did not provoke the accident by first pulling the tile from the floor intentionally and then tripping on it later.

It is, therefore, important that managers anticipate dangers and take the necessary precautions to eliminate accidents. This is best achieved by having a

safety committee—a small group of employees who, among other duties, inspects the property regularly for potentially dangerous hazards. A typical safety committee documents accidents that have occurred, provides for a well-stocked first-aid kit, recommends having a CPR-certified employee on duty, and has servers trained in the Heimlich maneuver in case someone begins to choke while eating in the restaurant. Typical examples of negligence cases causing injury to guests in hospitality establishments involve the following:

- Defective room furniture
- Electrical and heating hazards
- Surges in the shower hot water line that cause scalding
- Slip-and-fall accidents (usually because of slippery wet floors)
- Defective floor covers
- Objects on floors (a suitcase or orange peel)
- Spilling hot liquids on guests
- Poor lighting (indoors or outdoors)
- Swimming pool hazards
- Faulty fire suppression systems
- Ineffective security measures
- Falls caused by snow and ice on hotel grounds

CASE 15.3   Negligence in a Restaurant Setting

A patron left her table located in a dimly lit, elevated restaurant area and fell to the tile floor. According to her description, she landed in "a wet greasy puddle that was concealed in the darkness." The defendant restaurant contended that management had no knowledge of any foreign substance on the floor and that the patron failed to exercise ordinary care for safety.

The restaurant's manager on duty stated that food was continuously carried over the steps to the area where the injured party was seated and that the manager had inspected the entire restaurant 5 minutes before the accident. She further said that the restaurant had a policy for inspecting and cleaning the premises by the manager and servers, constantly monitoring for potential dangerous conditions, picking up and sweeping the floor as needed. A restaurant employee also stated that he had been waiting tables in the area of the accident and saw nothing on the floor within 5 minutes of the time the fall took place.

ASSIGNMENT: Discuss this case and suggest what the judgment might have been. Do you think that the restaurant's standing policy for floor inspections and cleaning had an effect on the outcome of the trial?

CASE 15.4 Negligence in a Banquet Room

A guest attending a national convention caught her foot on the leg of a chair, falling and injuring herself. The accident happened when the plaintiff was leaving a banquet room where, as she alleged, the long tables were too close to each other to leave adequate room between seated guests. The plaintiff stated that the distance between the tables was just 42 inches, with some tables having chairs back to back to those of the next table. At the time of the fall, the lights in the banquet room were dimmed, with a spotlight on the head table. Testimony indicated that servers were unable to move down the aisles between the long tables, the servers passing down the dishes from person to person from the end of the table. The defendant contended that there was no violation of any statute or ordinance.

ASSIGNMENT: Discuss this case and decide whether the injuries caused to the convention attendee were foreseeable by the hotel. Do you think that the setup of the room would have had anything to do with the judgment?

LIABILITY AND THE OPERATION OF RESTAURANTS AND BARS

As with lodging operations, restaurants and bars have a duty to provide reasonable safety and protection (both from other patrons and employees) for their customers. In addition, the law sets liability for serving adulterated or spoiled food and regulates the sale of alcoholic beverages. To avoid liability, restaurants must also fulfill the requests of guests for elimination of certain ingredients from food served. If the establishment fails to comply with the request and the patron becomes ill, the restaurant could be found liable. Requests of this type are frequently asked by people with allergies who have strong reactions to certain foods, such as peanuts, shrimp, or monosodium glutamate (MSG).

Restaurateurs must be particularly attentive to keep food at the right temperature to eliminate the risk of food-borne illnesses. Pathogenic bacteria, such as **salmonella**, **clostridium perfringens**, and **cocci**, can cause severe diseases. If it is proved in court that food caused an illness, a jury will most surely find the establishment liable for compensatory, and in some cases punitive, damages.

Several states have enacted **truth-in-menu laws**—legislation that seeks to eliminate untruthful statements of food ingredients by restaurants. For example, a restaurant cannot advertise frozen seafood as fresh or substitute imitation crabmeat for Dungeness.

CASE 15.5 Food Merchantability

A restaurant patron alleged that he had been served food that was supposedly unwholesome, adulterated, and not fit for human consumption. At 8 AM he had a breakfast that consisted of grapefruit sections, fried eggs, hash browns, a roll, and a cup of coffee. He had eaten lightly the day before because of a cholesterol test that was conducted an hour before his breakfast. The plaintiff stated that the eggs were on the cold side and did not taste right.

He began experiencing stomach pains and feeling nauseated at about 12:30 PM that day. He was admitted to the hospital at approximately 6 PM, where he was diagnosed with acute pancreatitis. The doctor's opinion was that the cause of the sickness was the food eaten at the restaurant, specifying that a hearty meal could bring on the symptoms of that disease. He also testified that fasting followed by a hearty meal could have brought on the pancreatitis. The doctor further stated that he was unable to confirm with certainty that the plaintiff consumed unwholesome food at the restaurant.

ASSIGNMENT: From the information at hand, discuss this case and suggest what the judgment might have been.

States also regulate the sale of alcoholic beverages, which if abused can cause diminished physical coordination and may lead to conflicts with or harassment of other individuals. One of the most strictly enforced regulations is that of not selling alcohol to underage patrons. Establishments are liable for heavy fines if operators do not enforce this rule. Likewise, lodging properties must not serve drinks in guest rooms or provide access to minibars to underage or visibly intoxicated guests or to patrons who are known to be habitually unruly.

The business will be subject to **third-party liability**—potential responsibility for any misdoing committed on or off the premises by an impaired patron. For example, the law will hold liable not only the drunk driver who causes a traffic accident but also the establishment where that person got visibly drunk. Many states have enacted **Dram Shop Acts**, laws imposing liability on an establishment that contributes to intoxication of individuals who cause injury to others or allows a potential driver to become visibly intoxicated.

There are several ways to prevent liability for alcohol misuse:

- Train bartenders and servers to identify patrons who have had too much to drink. Instruct them on how to cut drinkers off; if a dispute arises, support the servers in their decisions.
- Feature nonalcoholic beverages as an alternative to alcoholic drinks on the menu.
- Instruct bartenders and servers to card all patrons who look underage.
- Immediately stop any disorderly or offensive acts initiated by patrons who have had too much to drink. Failure to eject a quarrelsome person who subsequently causes injury to others in a fight may result in the establishment being found liable.

CASE 15.6 Alcohol Liability

A bar patron was a passenger in a car driven by his friend. The car crashed and the passenger suffered serious injuries. Both individuals had been drinking together before the accident in a nearby bar. The plaintiff testified that they had been purchasing pitchers of beer in rounds. The defense lawyer argued that buying such rounds amounted to buying drinks for the driver who caused the accident and, therefore, that the plaintiff was a noninnocent party under the Dram Shop Acts. The plaintiff argued that his participation in bringing about the intoxication should not preclude being compensated for damages by the licensee. The defense based its case on whether the plaintiff actively participated in the intoxication of the driver.

ASSIGNMENT: Based on the information given, discuss the case and suggest what the judgment might have been. Do you think the bar would have been found to be liable in this case?

CASE 15.7 Patron Protection from Injury

The plaintiff and her friend entered a restaurant and sat in a booth across from a group of six individuals already having dinner. People in the group began engaging in coarse conversation, aimed to be overheard and shock the plaintiff and her companion. At one point, the restaurant supervisor asked the group to quiet down, but the abusive shouting continued.

Later on, as the group was getting up to leave, one of the individuals directly insulted the plaintiff. After an exchange of affronts, the defendant struck the plaintiff on the face with a clenched fist, bruising her face and nose. The plaintiff called the attacker a racial expletive; this encouraged the attacker to strike the victim again. The restaurant supervisor stood by watching but did not intervene or call the police since he did not feel the situation warranted it.

As the fight continued, the plaintiff's friend ran to the counter to dial for help but was told by the supervisor that the phone was not for public use. Sometime later, he did call the police. The attacker and friends were scared away and left the area. When the police arrived, the supervisor said that the attacker had caused a few similar disturbances in the past. The plaintiff filed suit against the restaurant, alleging that management had failed to provide security measures to protect her.

ASSIGNMENT: Discuss this case and determine whether the restaurant was at fault. Did management act properly under the circumstances?

LAWS AND REGULATIONS AFFECTING EMPLOYMENT

Many lawsuits against hospitality establishments are related to employment procedures and employee-management relations. These cases can be initiated by workers or by government agencies that regulate employment issues. Because employment laws and regulations are constantly enacted or changed at federal, state, and local levels, hospitality managers should stay current with those in effect in their places of operation. The most important aspects of employment law deal with workers' wages, discrimination in the workplace, and working eligibility.

Fair Labor Standards Act

In 1938, a law known as the **Fair Labor Standards Act (FLSA)** was enacted to enforce provisions for minimum wages, overtime pay, equal pay for equal work, and child labor. The law requires payment to hourly workers of an hourly minimum wage established by Congress, although states may impose a higher minimum wage than the federal law determines. One exception to this requirement is the application of a percentage of tips received by workers toward the minimum wage. Another exception is the wages received for training when workers between the ages of 16 and 19 enter the workforce for the first time. The overtime pay regulation does not apply to supervisory positions that do not require performing hourly worker tasks and that are paid a stipulated fixed salary. Employees who are considered supervisors or managers usually meet the following conditions:

- Regularly directing the work of at least two other employees.
- Having the authority to hire and fire, or recommending hiring and firing, transferring, and promoting.
- Performing nonmanagerial duties that do not take more than 40 percent of work time.

The law requires that hourly employees working more than 40 hours per week receive at least one and one-half times their regular hourly wage. For example, an employee making $7.50 an hour should receive $11.25 when working overtime.

A provision of the FLSA establishes that men and women who perform the same tasks requiring the same skills and responsibility receive the same compensation. This law attempts to stop the common discriminatory practices in the workplace of paying women less than men are paid for the same type of work.

The FLSA establishes a minimum age for workers, restricts the number of hours and times minors can work, and limits the types of jobs they can perform. For example, children cannot start work as early and end their shift as late as adult workers can during the school year; young employees working in the kitchen are not allowed to run a slicing machine, mechanical mixers, or any equipment that is dangerous to operate.

Under the FLSA, employers must furnish uniforms and reimburse employees for uniform maintenance if the cost to an employee of purchasing and maintaining the uniform would cut into the employee's federal minimum wage. The Federal Wage and Hour Division estimates that the time spent in maintaining a uniform is about 1 hour a week.

A notice to employees outlining the FLSA must be posted where employees may easily see it. The notice may be obtained from regional offices of the Wage and Hour Division.

CASE 15.8   Overtime and Salaried Employees

A Massachusetts hospitality corporation with approximately 200 restaurants staffed its units with two to five management-level employees, including those with the title of associate manager. According to the plaintiff, most of the duties performed by associate managers involved tasks usually expected of hourly workers, such as preparing pizzas, sandwiches, salads, and other foods, running the cash register, waiting on customers, and cleaning the store. The defendant company stated that the purpose of the menial tasks was to "learn by doing." The company also argued that associate managers were considered "part of management at all times."

Although he was a manager in training, the plaintiff alleged that he regularly performed duties that did not involve supervision and that therefore he was entitled to receive overtime pay.

ASSIGNMENT: Discuss this case and suggest what the judgment might have been. Do you think the company was attempting to exploit their associate managers or was it trying to use the "learn by doing method" to train them?

DISCRIMINATION IN THE WORKPLACE

Discrimination in the workplace was transformed in 1964 by Title VII of the Civil Rights Act. Specifically, this statute forbids employers from discriminating in hiring, firing, and treating individuals in regard to compensation and other conditions of employment because of their race, color, religion, sex, or national origin. In 1991, the Americans with Disabilities Act (ADA) was enacted, aimed at providing equal opportunity to the disabled. In all cases, employers who discriminate may be liable for compensatory damages, including back pay and other monetary losses. If employers are found guilty of malicious illegal discrimination that violates an employee's rights, punitive damages may also be awarded for the emotional pain caused by the discrimination.

The Pregnancy Discrimination Act of Title VII states that it is unlawful to treat the medical condition associated with pregnancy and childbirth less favorably than other disabilities unless they cause interference with the normal conduct of business. The **Age Discrimination in Employment Act (ADEA)** is a federal law intended to prevent employers from discriminating against workers on the basis of age. The ADEA considers it unlawful to deny employment or to engage in discriminatory discharge because of a person's age.

There are a variety of behaviors that hospitality managers should avoid when dealing with discrimination issues:

- Giving preference to any social group, be it minority or majority.
- Preventing employees from wearing certain types of well-kept hairstyles, beards, or mustaches.
- Condoning racially derogatory remarks, jokes, or ethnic slurs.
- Rejecting employees looking for a job who are not fluent in English if this language is not a job requirement (for example, for a position as a dishwasher).
- Rejecting a legal alien applicant because of his or her accent, if it does not interfere with job performance.
- Refusing to provide reasonable accommodation for employee attendance at religious services if this does not interfere with work.
- Hiring one gender only, for example, in positions as servers or bartenders.
- Requiring one sex but not the other to wear a uniform if both sexes are performing the same job.
- Allowing unwelcome sexual advances to take place in the workplace.
- Failing to modify facilities to accommodate the needs of disabled employees.

In 1993, the federal government passed the **Family and Medical Leave Act (FMLA)**, which entitles workers to obtain leave time for family emergencies, such as childbirth, child care, caring for a close relative who has a serious health problem, and adoption of a child. Employees returning from such a leave must be reinstated to the same positions, or equivalent ones, that they held before the leave took place. There are some regulations regarding a worker's eligibility, such as a minimum of hours worked per year.

WORK ELIGIBILITY OF JOB APPLICANTS

The law protects American citizens and legal foreign residents in the United States from discrimination in the workplace. Because statutes on discrimination are applicable to employee recruiting, selecting, and hiring, hospitality managers must make sure not to commit any illegal actions during these functions, for example, advertising a position for people under 40 only. Managers must also not ask unlawful questions on the application form or during the interview, such as "Do you observe religious holidays?" or "Do you intend to have children in the future?"

Immigration laws prohibit illegal aliens from working in the United States, requiring employers to verify working eligibility for all job applicants. Employers are required by the Immigration Reform and Control Act of 1986 to have applicants fill out Form I-9 and produce documentation of personal identity and legal status. Examples of documents that establish individual identity are a driver's license or U.S. military card; examples of documents that establish employment eligibility are a Social Security card or a U.S. birth certificate. Turning away potential employees because of a foreign accent or appearance is illegal.

CASE 15.9   Discrimination in the Workplace

The plaintiff, a 45-year-old worker at an inn, alleged that his employer terminated him on the basis of his age. The manager of the defendant property testified that the work performed by the plaintiff had been satisfactory. The evidence shown in court indicated that the inn's manager wanted to replace the claimant with a younger employee. To this effect, he placed ads in the local newspaper urging "young, energetic persons to apply" for the position.

Under questioning, the manager testified that when the plaintiff offered to learn additional tasks for his job, if that was considered necessary, the defendant replied that "you cannot teach old dogs new tricks."

ASSIGNMENT: Discuss this case and suggest what the decision of the court most likely was. Did the manager behave in violation of federal law?

KEY CONCEPTS/TERMS

administrative law
Age Discrimination in Employment
   Act (ADEA)
Americans with Disabilities Act
   (ADA)
breach of contract
civil law
clostridium perfringens
cocci
common law
compensatory damages
constitutional law
criminal law
defendant
discrimination
Dram Shop Acts
Fair Labor Standards Act (FLSA)

Family and Medical Leave Act
   (FMLA)
fraud
lock out
negligence
ordinance
plaintiff
precedent
punitive damages
safety committee
salmonella
statutes
statutory law
third-party liability
tort
truth-in-menu laws

Epilogue

Having completed this course, you should now be prepared to begin your career in the hospitality industry. As with all degrees, a degree in hotel and restaurant management is a good start for learning about the field, but there is much more you will discover as you deal with on-the-job challenges. For this reason, don't be too critical about your first position, even if it is nothing like the job you dreamed of. Everything you learn from it will help you as you move through your career.

In order to succeed, you will have to work hard, gain operating experience, and make wise career choices. In restaurant operations, you will probably be asked to work in every front- and back-of-the-house job before being promoted to unit general manager. In lodging operations, your first positions as manager-trainee and junior supervisor may eventually lead to your becoming manager of a department. Your objective then should be to work your way up to the position of resident manager, a critical step to becoming GM of a large establishment. In all cases, your personal and managerial abilities, as they are perceived by your superiors, will be the determining factor for your career success.

The personal characteristics of successful hoteliers are the same as those shown by executives in other business professions. Good analytical skills are necessary to grasp the crux of every situation at hand; a confident, dynamic, decisive personality is needed to successfully resolve the multiple challenges common in everyday operations; a good understanding of interpersonal relations, coupled with a sincere wish to understand others, is important. Being perceived by subordinates as an honest, fair, and trustful manager is also critical. Successful hospitality executives are goal-oriented, flexible, ethical, entrepreneurial, and unafraid of change and of taking risks.

Early success for young hospitality managers can be exciting, even glamorous. It is for this reason that temptations may arise and eventually undermine personal lives and even careers. Excessive alcohol, rich foods, long work hours with neither adequate exercise nor relaxation, and inattention to family—all are traps into which it is easy for the hotelier to fall.

Keep your life in balance. Enjoy your work. And may you have much success.

Glossary

Accounts payable   Amounts due to creditors.

Accounts receivable   Amounts due from guests and customers.

Administrative law   Laws enacted by government organizations intended to regulate a specific trade, such as the safety of foods and pharmaceutical products by the Food and Drug Administration agency.

Age Discrimination in Employment Act (ADEA)   A federal law intended to prevent employers from discriminating against workers on the basis of age.

À la carte   A menu or items on a menu where individual dishes are listed and priced separately.

À la minute   A dish prepared at the time it is ordered.

Americans with Disabilities Act (ADA)   A law passed in 1991 mandating the elimination of discrimination against individuals with disabilities.

Ampere   The unit that measures an electric current's strength.

Aperitif   A fortified wine, such as sherry and vermouth, often flavored with herbs and spices and served as an opener to a meal.

Assets   Property or resources owned by businesses.

Auditories   In communication, individuals who tend to map their cognitions from sounds.

Autocratic style   A leadership style in which managers make decisions alone or with little input from subordinates.

Average daily rate (ADR)   The average price of guest rooms during a given period of time. The rate is obtained by dividing room revenue by the number of rooms sold.

Average inventory   A listing of average quantities of food or beverage.

Balance sheet   A statement showing owners' equity (assets − liabilities), indicating the financial position of the company at a given point.

Balancing up   A financial calculation of the day's transactions done by the night auditor in lodging operations.

Banquet kitchen   A separate kitchen where banquet dishes are prepared or assembled.

Basic charge   Minimum amount charged by utility companies regardless of consumption.

Béarnaise sauce   A butter and egg yolk reduction containing tarragon; usually served with grilled meat.

Béchamel sauce   A white sauce made with milk and a white roux.

Bed linens   Washable linen used on beds such as sheets and pillowcases.

Benchmarking   Comparison of a company's costs of performing a business activity with the costs incurred by other companies for the same activity in order to ascertain competitiveness.

Beurre manié   A thickening paste made of one part butter and one part flour.

Beverage revenue   The revenue obtained from selling beverages.

Boiler   A closed vessel in which hot water or steam is generated.

Bonus system   Monetary incentives for workers to reward productivity in the workplace.

Brandy   A distilled liquor made of grapes and other fruits.

Breach of contract   An act that in truth and fairness defeats the essential purposes of the parties to a contract.

Breakout room   A small conference room.

Burgundy   In the United States, the generic red house wine served in an establishment. It is also a wine-producing region in southeast France.

Business collusion   A secret business agreement for a fraudulent purpose.

Butler service   Personalized service provided by upscale properties; similar to the floor-concierge service.

Cancellation   The act of rescinding a reservation for a guest room or function.

Capital accounts   The shares owned by a company.

Carafe   A glass container often used to serve house wines.

Career services   An office in most colleges and universities in charge of helping students find a job. Students should contact this office as early as possible in their senior year.

Cash bar   Drink service usually set up in banquet functions where guests pay cash to the bartender or use tickets previously purchased from a cashier.

Cash flow   A company's cash budget.

Casual dining   Relaxed food service.

Chablis   In the United States, the generic white house wine served in an establishment. It is also a wine-producing area in France's Burgundy region.

Château potatoes   Potatoes cooked gently in clarified butter until golden.

Chef de rang   A server in charge of a restaurant table section.

Cherries Jubilée   A dessert made with cherries, usually cooked and lighted table side, with thickened syrup and heated kirsch.

Chief executive officer (CEO)   The person responsible for a company's strategy, goal setting, and policy implementation.

Choron sauce   Béarnaise sauce with blended tomato paste.

City ledger   The accounts receivable at the front desk of nonregistered guests or entities that use hotel services on credit.

Civil law   The law that applies in cases involving wrongs done to individuals.

Cleaning supplies   The products and utensils used in cleaning.

Closing balance   The balance of all accounts for the day's business cycle that is brought forward as opening balance for the next day's business cycle. The closing balance consists of the opening balance plus the day's charges, minus the day's credits received.

Clostridium perfringens   Pathogenic bacteria that can cause severe food-borne diseases.

Cocci   Pathogenic bacteria capable of causing infectious diseases.

Code of ethics   A company's system of rules of behavior founded on moral principles.

Coercive power   A type of leadership power in which a manager compels subordinates to perform a task under the threat of punishment.

Coil   A continuous pipe forming spirals or rings through which cold or hot water or steam is circulated for refrigeration or heating purposes.

Commis de rang   In fine restaurants, a helper of the chef de rang.

Common law   Legal rules based on previous court decisions, customs, and practices.

Compensatory damages   A sum of money to cover the loss experienced by a plaintiff.

Compressor   In refrigeration, a machine, usually driven by electricity by which a gas is compressed so that it can be condensed at desired temperatures.

Consolidated P&L statement   A report that encompasses the operational results of all the departments of a property.

Consolidated room sales statement   The projection of room sales for a fiscal year.

Constitutional law   The law embodied in the fundamental principles of the U.S. Constitution.

Consultative style   A leadership style used by a manager to get ideas and suggestions from subordinates prior to making decisions.

Controlling   A management function aimed at measuring actual with expected standards established during the planning process and effecting necessary corrections if deviations from the standards are found.

Coolant gas   A gas, usually Freon, used as a refrigerating agent.

Cost-based rate   The average rate calculated on the basis of the initial cost of a property plus the projected return on investment.

Costing the recipe   A calculation of the cost of ingredients to determine the price of a drink.

Cost of sales   The cost of food or beverage used in a given period of time.

Cost per occupied room   The average cost spent per room; usually applies to guest supplies.

Cover letter   A letter sent with a resumé to potential employers.

Criminal law   A classification of the law in which the wrong is considered to be committed against society at large and involves violation of a criminal statue.

Current month   In budgets and P&L statements, the operational projections or results for a month in question.

Curriculum vitae   A written document describing in detail the education, work-related history, and qualifications that a job-seeker possesses; an extensive resumé.

Cutoff date   The designated date when the reservation of a block of rooms must be released by the buyer to the establishment.

Cycle menu   A series of menus that rotate over a period of time to eventually repeat itself.

Daiquiri   A sweet-sour mixed drink usually made with rum, lime juice, sugar, and syrup.

Day guest   A guest who uses a guest room for part of the day only.

Decentralized system   In heating and air conditioning, using individual units (rather than a large single unit) to heat or cool rooms.

Declining-balance depreciation   A method of depreciation whereby higher amounts of depreciation expense are recorded in the earlier years of an asset's life.

Defendant   The person or entity accused.

Demand rate   The demand for electricity at a certain time. Usually, the demand rate is lower during the night and higher during the day.

Democratic style   Leadership style used by managers who prefer to involve subordinates in the decision-making process.

Departmental budget   Operational projections for a specific department.

Dessert wine   A fortified, often sweet and rich wine such as Port and cream sherry; served at the end of a meal.

Dining room captain   In fine restaurants, a server in charge of a table section; equivalent to the chef de rang position.

Direct bill   Account receivable bills in the city ledger to be paid by an entity rather than by the person or persons who originated the charges.

Directing   A management function aimed at achieving the goals of a company or operational unit.

Direct question   In interviewing, a question usually beginning with what, when, where, who, or why.

Discrimination   Differentiating in favor of or against a person or persons because of race, religion, gender, or age.

Downsizing   A management practice aimed at minimizing operational costs by reducing organizational layers of supervision.

Dram Shop Acts   Laws enacted by states imposing liability on an establishment that contributes to the intoxication of individuals who may cause injury to others.

Dubarry   Cooked or garnished with cauliflower.

Duct   In most cases, a conduit through which cold or hot air is circulated.

Dumbwaiter   A small elevator used to send food and equipment to service stations located in the upper floors of a building.

Earning statement   Another name for the profit and loss statement.

Eggs Benedict   Poached eggs on half an English muffin topped with Canadian bacon and hollandaise sauce.

Empathy   The appreciative perception or understanding of another person.

Empowerment   A management approach that gives employees the necessary authority to provide effective customer service.

En papillote   Food cooked in its own juice in an envelope or bag.

Entrée   The main course of a meal.

E-shaped room setup   A table set up in the shape of the letter E.

Espagnole sauce   A classic brown sauce made with browned beef or veal bones, dark stock, tomato, mirepoix, and flour.

Estimated direct expenses   Projected operational expenses.

Estimated revenue   Projected revenue for a specific period of time.

Ethical dilemma   A situation requiring a choice between equally undesirable alternatives leading to a clash of ethical principles.

Ethnic restaurant   A restaurant that specializes in foods originally from a certain country or region.

Evening team   A housekeeping team in charge of cleaning functions in the evening, after the regular teams have clocked out.

Executive committee   In large properties, the directors in charge of divisions. For example, the rooms division and F&B division directors are members of the executive committee.

Executive officer   A manager in charge of setting the strategic planning of a business or corporation.

Extemporaneous speaking   Speaking on the spur of the moment without preparation or notes.

Fair Labor Standards Act (FLSA)   A law that enforces provisions for minimum wages, overtime pay, equal pay for equal work, and child labor.

Family and Medical Leave Act (FMLA)   A federal law entitling workers to obtain leave time for family emergencies, such as childbirth, child care, caring for a close relative who has a serious health problem, and adoption of a child.

Family restaurant   A restaurant offering dishes that appeal to families. It often includes a children's and senior's menu.

Field sales   The solicitation and bookings of business door to door.

Fillet   A boneless cut from meat tenderloin or a full-length side of fish removed from its central bone.

Financial objectives   Goals for monetary receipts or expenditures set by a business or corporation.

Fiscal year   Any 12-month period at the end of which a firm determines its financial condition without regard to the calendar year.

Fixed assets   Long-term capital assets that are depreciated over a number of years.

Fixed budget   A budget based on only one level of sales instead of being based on sales broken down month by month.

Fixed team   A housekeeping cleaning team scheduled to clean public areas regardless of the property's occupancy.

Flip chart   A large paper pad mounted on an easel.

Flow controller   A device placed in shower heads to reduce water flow.

Food cost   The cost of the edible products purchased for the preparation of food. The food cost percentage is obtained by dividing the food cost by the revenue from food sales.

Food revenue   The revenue obtained from food sales. The food revenue is obtained by multiplying the number of covers sold by the average check.

Fortified wine   A wine that has a spirit, usually brandy, added to make it stronger.

Franchised property   An establishment that has acquired the right to use the name and services of a hospitality chain.

Fraud   Deceit, trickery, or breach of confidence to gain an unfair or dishonest advantage.

French cuisine   A cooking style featuring dishes and cooking methods usually originating in France.

Furnace   A structure in which to generate heat. Commonly, the apparatus that burns natural gas to generate hot air that is distributed by way of a blower.

Garniture   A food addition to a finished dish to add visual appeal, color, or flavor, such as a sprig of watercress served with a grilled T-bone steak.

Ghost flush   An internal loss of water in toilet tanks.

Gross profit   In a restaurant budget or income statement, the amount resulting from subtracting the cost of sales from the total sales.

Guest amenities   Complimentary supplies provided to guests.

Guest folio   A guest's bill.

Guest ledger   All accounts receivable of guests staying in a property.

Guest supplies   Complimentary items provided for guests.

Heat pump   A device that uses the refrigeration cycle to provide heat by reversing the direction of the refrigerant flow, which causes the evaporator and condenser parts to switch functions.

Heat transfer   The loss of heat or conditioned air when a difference of temperatures exists between two spaces.

Heat-transmission coefficient   A number that determines the insulation capability of a substance or structure as measured in Btu per hour per square foot in degrees Fahrenheit.

Hertz   A unit for measuring current or sound vibrations per second.

Hollandaise sauce   A reduction of egg yolks and clarified butter with lemon juice.

Horsepower   A unit for measuring power, or rate of work, equivalent to 550 foot-pounds per second.

Hospitality suite   A room or suite set aside for entertaining guests.

Host bar   Drink service in which guests are not charged but the host pays for all drinks consumed.

Houseperson   A worker in charge of general jobs in the housekeeping or banquet departments.

House wine   Generic wine usually sold by the glass or in carafes. Typical American house wines are Burgundy (red), Chablis (white), and rosé (pink).

Impromptu speaking   Speaking before a group without previous preparation.

Incidental charges   Charges that are not included on a master bill but that are to be paid directly by individual guests.

Income   The operating results of a business for a period of time.

Income statement   A financial report showing the operating results of a business for a period of time.

Independently owned company   A privately owned operation that is not part of a hospitality chain.

Inside sales   Sales efforts directed to house guests; merchandising.

Interdepartmental credit   Credit given to a department for the use of products used by another department. The cost of a bottle of beer used by the kitchen to make beer-batter is credited to "beverage" and debited to "food."

Job fair   A presentation, usually organized and sponsored by a college's career services office, where prospective employers display their job offers to students about to graduate.

Junior suite   A large room in which the bedroom is separated from a small living room by a partition.

Kilowatt   One thousand watts.

Kinesthetics   In communication, individuals who perceive facts better from feelings.

Kirschwasser   A brandy distilled from wild dark cherries.

Labor productivity   The amount of labor it takes to produce a certain level of output.

Laissez-faire style   A leadership style used by managers who allow employees to make work decisions on their own.

Liabilities   The debt or obligation of a company.

Life span   The working life of fixed assets, usually expressed in number of years.

Line cook   A cook working the kitchen line or serving counter.

Leading question   In interviewing, a question that can usually be answered with "yes" or "no."

Letter of agreement   A document signed by a buyer accepting an accommodation or function proposal.

Listening   In communication, a skill that is critical to determine the needs, problems, and moods of the person who speaks.

List of references   A list of three or four individuals who know a job applicant well that is submitted to prospective employers along with a resumé.

Lock out   An act that prevents access to a guest by locking the door of his or her room.

Long-term debt   A liability or obligation to be paid off more than 1 year hence.

Low season   The time of the year during which business is at its lowest level.

Management company   A hospitality company hired by the owner of an establishment to manage operations.

Management team   In housekeeping, the employees who manage the department. Usually, in large properties, a team consists of the executive housekeeper, the housekeeping manager, and the laundry manager.

Market-based rate   The average rate of guest rooms based on the prices that the market can bear.

Market research   A study conducted before opening a hospitality establishment to identify the concept to be adopted based on the needs of the area's customers.

Marsala   A fortified dessert wine served at the end of a meal; also used in cooking.

Master account   The folio on which all group charges are posted.

Meeting planner   The person employed by corporations, organizations, or entities to book conventions and other functions.

Merchandising   The selling efforts conducted in an establishment.

Mise en place   The preparation of foods made ready before cooking or serving dishes.

Multi-unit chain   A hospitality chain operating several establishments.

Napped   Coated with a sauce.

Nature tourism   Tourism aimed at visiting natural attractions, such as Arizona's Grand Canyon.

Negligence   An act of carelessness committed by a person or entity that causes harm to an individual or individuals.

News release   Information provided to the press for publication. News releases are usually free of charge.

Nonreusable guest supplies   Items such as soaps that are used by guests only once.

Nonverbal behavior   In communication, gestures that serve as expressions of emotion.

No-show   A person or persons who have failed to register as scheduled.

Nouvelle cuisine   A modern cooking style (as distinguished from a classical style) in which unusual fresh ingredients, such as berries, tropical fruits, and exotic vegetables, are used. The term implies that the food is healthier than if cooked following classical recipes, which may use more fats, sugar, and refined grains.

Occupancy costs   Costs not related to operations, such as a property's mortgage.

Off-peak hours   The hours of the day when electricity consumption is lowest.

Older travelers   That segment of the tourist industry comprised of senior citizens.

On-call workers   Employees who can be called to work when needed. Typical on-call workers in the hospitality industry are banquet servers and bartenders.

On-peak hours   The hours of the day when electricity consumption is highest.

Open-ended question   In interviewing, a question that needs to be answered with, at least, one or several sentences, not simply yes or no.

Opening balance   The accounts receivable amount brought forward from the previous day's business cycle.

Opening team   The employees selected by a company to open a new establishment.

Operating expenses   In restaurant accounting, the costs of operations, excluding the cost of food and beverage.

Operating statement   Another name for the profit and loss report.

Opportunities   In SWOT analysis, the external opportunities that exist in a particular business environment.

Ordinance   A law enacted by local governments.

Organizing   A management function that coordinates the internal functioning of the workplace and establishes a pattern of relationships with other operational units.

Output   The productivity results of a worker or group of workers.

Overbooking   Taking a larger number of reservations than rooms are available for the same period.

Overstay   A guest who decides to stay beyond the scheduled date of departure.

Owner's equity   The net worth of a property, calculated as total assets minus total liabilities.

Packaging   Combining rooms and complementary or discounted services into a single-price offering.

Panaché de légumes   A vegetable medley.

Par   The ideal number of items to have in stock.

Participative style   A leadership style in which managers prefer to get ideas and suggestions from subordinates.

Pastis   A strong liqueur used in France as an aperitif. Pernod is a well-known liqueur of this type.

Personal power   A power that is based on managers influencing employees through their behavior and personality.

Personal selling   Sales efforts conducted either by telephone or face-to-face.

Physical inventory   The actual counting and pricing of assets.

Plaintiff   The wronged party who brings suit in a court of law.

Planning   The function of management aimed at setting objectives and developing strategies to achieve them.

Position power   A power over subordinates that is based on the manager's position in an organization.

Potage   A soup naturally thickened by a purée of its major ingredients.

Power factor   The time at which volts and amperes reach their peak or maximum values.

Precedent   A court decision that constitutes the basis for future cases.

Preregistration   Preassignment of rooms by the establishment to be available on the guests' arrival. Preregistered guests do not need to go through check-in procedures.

Press conference   An event in which information of interest to the general public is released by an establishment to the media.

Productivity   The work output of a worker or group of workers.

Productivity standard   The average output of workers during a fixed period of time—for example, cleaning 16 guest rooms per shift in the housekeeping department.

Profit and loss (P&L) statement   A financial report showing amounts earned from sales of goods and services, less costs incurred, for a certain period of time. Also called *earnings statement, income statement, and operating statement.*

Profit before occupancy costs   The profit made from operations.

Publicity   Public relations efforts conducted by an establishment to release relevant information to the media.

Punitive damages   Any sum awarded to a nonbreaching party in excess of compensatory damages.

Quick service restaurant   A restaurant where customers are served immediately.

Rack rate   A regular, not discounted, rate.

Rapport   In communication, the ability to communicate effectively while making others comfortable.

Réchaud   A small heated stand where finished dishes are kept warm.

Reservations bucket   In noncomputerized operations, the enclosure or container where the reservations are filed.

Resistance   In electricity, the property of a conductor by which the passage of a current is opposed, causing electric energy to be transformed into heat.

Resumé   An abbreviated account of a job-seeker's education, job experience, and qualifications.

Return on investment (ROI)   A ratio obtained by dividing profit by the owner's investment.

Reward power   A type of leadership power in which managers persuade subordinates to perform a job by offering something in return.

Reward system   A method of compensating workers according to their work productivity.

Rooms division   The division in charge of servicing guest rooms. Typically, the rooms division consists of the housekeeping and front office departments.

Room setup   The specific arrangement of a room for a meeting or other function.

Rosé   Pink or blush wine. A well-known rosé wine is produced in the Anjou region of France.

Roux   A thickening agent made by blending together flour and a fat (usually butter) over low heat.

Roving mike   A hand microphone that allows a speaker to roam about the stage or interact with the audience.

Safety committee   A small group of employees who inspect a property regularly for potentially dangerous hazards, among other duties.

Sales blitz   Targeting a specific area with great concentration for a short period of time.

Salmonella   A family of disease-producing bacteria.

Section housekeeper   The worker in charge of servicing a section of guest rooms.

Section housekeeper workload   The specific number of guest rooms a section housekeeper is assigned per regular shift.

Service bar   A bar that prepares drinks for table service and is often not open to the public.

Sherry A wine, fortified with a spirit (usually brandy), used as an aperitif or dessert drink, and in cooking.

Short-term budget A budget prepared for a short period of time, generally less than a year.

Shoulder season The period between high and low seasons.

Situational question In interviewing, a question asking about a hypothetical situation.

Sommelier A wine steward.

Sous-chef A kitchen supervisor reporting to the executive chef.

Special-interest traveler A visitor interested in a specific tourism offer or attraction—for example, someone interested in bird-watching.

Standing mike A microphone attached to a metal stand or rostrum.

Status quo The state in which anything was or is without change.

Statutes Federal and state laws and regulations.

Statutory law Laws promulgated by legislators and endorsed by executives (from the president to state governors and mayors).

Straight-line depreciation A method of calculating depreciation whereby equal portions of the cost of a fixed asset are shown as an expense for each year of its expected life.

Strategic mission A statement providing an organization with an identity in regard to business emphasis and path for development.

Strategic objectives A series of performance targets, results, and outcomes that an organization sets to accomplish.

Strategic vision The roadmap for a company's short- and long-term future.

Strengths In SWOT analysis, the internal effective properties an establishment or company possesses.

Suggestive selling A selling technique in which products or services are advertised or displayed in-house.

SWOT analysis A classic operational strategic planning model. The acronym represents the four key concepts of this strategy: (1) strengths, (2) weaknesses, (3) opportunities, and (4) threats.

Table d'hôte menu A single-priced series of dishes served as a whole meal.

Team supervisor In housekeeping, the person in charge of supervising a certain number of section housekeepers.

Terry cloth Bathroom linens in guest rooms, usually towels, washcloths, and bath mats.

Theater-style room setup A room arrangement in which chairs are placed side-by-side in separate aisles.

Therm A unit equal to 100,000 Btu.

Third-party liability Potential liability under the Dram Shop Acts in which a vendor of alcoholic beverages may be found liable by those who are injured from the patron's intoxication.

Threats In SWOT analysis, the external difficulties existing in the business environment.

Toastmasters International   An organization whose goal is to improve the speaking skills of its members.

Tomato sauce   Any red sauce made from stock thickened with tomato purée and/or roux.

Tone of voice   In communication, the volume of voice used to communicate.

Tort   A wrongful act that injures another person.

Total food consumed   The sum of all food used during a certain period of time, including interdepartmental transfers and spoilage.

Total quality management (TQM)   A theory that emphasizes the achievement of guest satisfaction by empowering employees to make service decisions on their own.

Tournedos   A thin slice (medallion) of beef tenderloin.

Truth in menu laws   Legislation that seeks to eliminate untruthful statements of food ingredients by restaurants.

Understay   The departure of a guest before his or her scheduled checkout date.

Undocumented alien   An illegal resident, usually an individual without a permit to work in the United States.

Upselling   Efforts made by sales agents or reservationists to obtain the highest possible price or room rate.

Variance analysis   The comparison of budgeted figures with actual results.

Velouté   Blond sauce made of veal, chicken, or fish stock.

Verbal factors   In communication, the words spoken and the tone of voice used.

Vermouth   A fortified wine used as an aperitif or combined with liquor to make mixed drinks.

Véronique   A dish (usually poached fillet of sole) containing a glazed fish fumet and garnished with Muscatel grapes.

VIP   An acronym used to identify a very important person; a distinguished guest.

Visuals   In communication, individuals who prefer to use picture words, such as "I see what you mean" or "it looks good to me."

Voice rate   In communication, the number of words expressed in a certain period of time.

Volt   The unit of electromotive force.

Voltage   Electromotive force reckoned or expressed in volts.

Walk a guest   To reject a guest who has a reservation because of overbooking.

Walking survey   An inspection conducted on site.

Water-cooling tower   A structure where water flowing from the condenser is cooled off so that it can be recycled back to the condenser.

Weaknesses   In SWOT analysis, the internal defects a company or establishment has or the internal difficulties it faces.

Weekend traveler   That segment of the tourist market usually composed of families who travel on weekends for leisure purposes.

Year to date   In budgets and P&L statements, the figures of any category expressed to date since the beginning of the fiscal year.

Yield management   A revenue maximization technique that aims to increase net yields by allocating available room capacity at optimum price.

Index